For Ammerdown.

David Reeves.

28ᵗʰ March 2015

Memoirs of a Very Dangerous Man

Memoirs of a Very Dangerous Man

DONALD REEVES

continuum

Continuum International Publishing Group

The Tower Building

11 York Road

London

SE1 7NX

80 Maiden Lane

Suite 704

New York

NY 10038

www.continuumbooks.com

First published 2009

British Library Cataloguing-in-Publication Data
A catalogue record for this book is available from the British Library.

ISBN 9781847063137

Typeset by BookEns Ltd, Royston, Herts.
Printed and bound by MPG Books Ltd., Bodmin, Cornwall

In memory of my mother and father

Contents

Acknowledgements

'At least you won't have to do any research,' said Charles Handy, friend, writer and social philosopher.

These words have been a constant reminder that *A Very Dangerous Man* is a personal story. Except for a short foray into the Church of England for which I have worked over thirty-five years, this book is not a story of institutions or organizations I have either started or with which I have been associated.

I am sure many of my colleagues would see things differently. Some may be surprised to see they are not mentioned. But I decided to be sparing with names. In all, twenty-eight priests, some full time, some part time, some retired, passed through the doors of the two parishes where I was the incumbent: St Peter's Morden and St James's Piccadilly, the latter not being a clergy dominated community. Many people gave time to work in cramped and difficult conditions in Piccadilly. To write about them all would mean a different sort of book, an ecclesiastical soap opera: *Rectory*.

But there is one person I need to acknowledge with special gratitude: my secretary Linda Maude. Linda arrived as a temp at Morden and stayed with me for the next twenty years. More than a secretary, she was PA and gate-keeper. She knew more about me than anyone else, put up with my frequently excessive demands and became the parish anchor.

Parts of this story are well documented elsewhere, particularly the Soul of Europe's activities in the Balkans, the Urban Ministry Project and St James's Piccadilly. My successor at Piccadilly, Charles

Hedley, said: 'You took all the papers and left the people.' To which I could only reply: 'Better that than the other way round.'

I kept a diary intermittently and this diary has jogged my memories.

I am also grateful to the archivist of St Paul's Cathedral, the librarians at the Athenaeum, Lambeth Palace library, the Wrexham Archive Service, the *Church Times* and West Sussex Records for prompt and helpful responses to my queries.

Then there are those who have encouraged me in this project, particularly Trevor Beeson, Geoffrey Court, Phillip Cowell, Neil Fair, Nicholas Frayling, Kate Goslett, Charles and Liz Handy, Godfrey Honeywill, John Holliman, Una Kroll, Peter Lewis, Paul Morris, Patrick Rohde, Jeremy Seabrook, Gillian Weir and Susan Wright. I apologize to all those many who have also encouraged and helped me and whose names I have not mentioned. I am grateful to Robin Baird Smith of Continuum for his encouragement and advice.

Andrew Barr and Peter Pelz gave much time correcting and editing the manuscript. I thank them for their counsel and attention during the writing of *A Very Dangerous Man*. Without Peter Pelz the course of my life would have been quite different.

Meanwhile responsibility for the book is mine and mine alone.

Introduction

Margaret Thatcher, Prime Minister, telephoned Enoch Powell in the summer of 1983 before he visited St James's Church Piccadilly where I was rector.

We were to take part in the radio programme *Any Questions?* The Prime Minister told him: 'Donald Reeves is a very dangerous man.' He relayed this comment to me, adding: 'I don't think you are dangerous at all.'

Had I been as dangerous as the prime minister said I would have been banned and silenced. Like many public figures I regularly received death threats, usually in red biro on lined paper.

This memoir explains why the prime minister was provoked. I have been called 'maverick', 'turbulent priest', 'traitor', 'communist', 'apostate', 'the Devil', 'interfering', 'red parson of Piccadilly', and more kindly: 'enigmatic', 'entrepreneur', 'impresario', 'visionary with attitude', 'priest of the Apocalypse' and 'the most extraordinary clergyman in the Church of England'.

Readers will be able to judge for themselves.

PART ONE

Beginnings

In 1939 the prospect of an invasion along the Sussex coastal plain persuaded my parents to send me away to boarding school. We lived outside the city of Chichester. I was five years old. At Branksome Hilders, a prep school near Haslemere in Surrey, 'in the hills' beyond the South Downs, I would be safe.

Boarding schools in those days were reckoned to provide the best preparation for life. The regime 'toughened you up', made you self-sufficient and self-reliant. I belonged to the generation that encouraged a stiff upper lip.

My abrupt departure at an early age felt like an amputation. The notion of home vanished, the trunk forever packed, unpacked and re-packed, a portable school boy's coffin.

Being parents did not come easy to my mother and father. I remembered my father as passive, taciturn and private. We always shook hands as though we had just been introduced. I knew little about him. When he grew older I hoped he might open up and tell me more about his life. One of the pleasures for me as a young vicar would be visiting residential homes and listening to stories of elderly women, describing high points in their lives, such as seeing Queen Victoria stopping at Mitcham Junction in the Royal Train ('a grumpy little old woman!').

Talking about the past did not interest my father and he vouchsafed nothing about himself. My own researches revealed he had been brought up in a seventeenth-century manor house, Croesnewyd

Hall near Wrexham, rented by my grandfather, a gentleman farmer who late in life married a much younger woman and started a family. My father's sister died young. His brother Sidney became the black sheep of the family. I remember Sidney having a broad Lancashire accent. Being the older brother he inherited the family fortune, which he then squandered on gambling, ending his life as a night watchman at Blackpool Bus Station. My mother particularly resented his selling off the furniture at Croesnewyd to pay his debts. 'He's a ne'er do well!' she told me. Years later I visited his widow, then living on a Blackpool housing estate. Her first words on opening the door to me were: 'If you've come for money there isn't any! And what I've got I'm leaving to a cat's home!' Then she shut the door in my face.

My father was educated at home before going to Cranwell in 1916, then on to a training school for the Royal Naval Air Reserve.

I came across a large heavy Bible printed in 1868 and showed it to my father. He paused for a long time before saying: 'We used to have prayers with the servants every morning.' And that was all I ever got out of him.

Cars and motor boats were my father's sole passions. He described himself as a garage proprietor and marine engineer. Nothing pleased him more than making engines purr and run smoothly.

He owned a garage in Chichester. With a small private income he had no interest in making money. The garage became his life. Under a snapshot of my father bending over the bonnet of a Morris 8 my mother's caption reads: 'Bill doing the usual.'

My mother was energetic, lively and gregarious, the eldest of a family of three sisters and one brother. Her father, a farm manager, died young leaving my grandmother to bring up the family at Tangmere near Chichester. With some family money my mother, her sisters and brother were educated privately. My uncle inherited a farm, and on leaving school my aunts became domestic companions, not quite members of the family, but more than just nannies.

The family revolved round Grandmother Rusbridger and I became her first and favourite grandchild. She liked my father, respecting his reticence and good manners.

After marriage my mother designed an unusual three-bedroom house with a spacious south-facing sitting room and a large kitchen, set in an acre of woodland two miles outside Chichester. If the family grew, the house could be extended. This did not happen. I remained the only child.

Temperamentally my parents were ill matched. My mother craved more out of life. She loved socializing, especially with male company. Even after I was born and up to 1939, my parents went on lengthy driving tours all over Europe with two close friends who were my godfathers.

A succession of nannies looked after me while they were gone. Sometimes I stayed with Grandmother Rusbridger. My aunt Anne, her youngest daughter, enjoyed telling me later that the first time my parents delivered me to her house I stared at everyone and wet my trousers. Another family memory, gleefully narrated by my mother, involved my christening. Preparations were made and at the party before the service drinks flowed until my parents realized they were running late. Everyone rushed to the church. They arrived, settled down and suddenly looked at each other: 'Where's the baby?'

Despite being passed around like a parcel from my grandmother to my aunts as they began to marry and have families of their own I preferred not being at home. I loved my grandmother, patient, kindly, old-fashioned and sometimes stern. I felt safe with her as she taught me how to tie my shoe-laces and knot my tie. At Christmas the whole family would gather at Hunston Manor, a sixteenth-century modest manor house owned by the Church Commissioners along with the farm that went with it. My uncle was the tenant farmer. No one went to church. Sitting under the big dining room table while everyone played roulette I would try to match the legs with the owners. Until leaving Chichester in 1957 my happiest memories were of visiting my aunts and uncles. I never enjoyed returning home. What was there to come home to?

War upset our fragile family unit. My father joined the Royal Naval Voluntary Reserve. He sailed up and down the English Channel in Motor Torpedo boats and had particular responsibility for ensuring the boats' engines functioned at their best. Emotionally he had always been absent from home; now he was physically absent.

My mother took over the business and ran the car as a hospital taxi. This ensured she could buy fuel, then heavily rationed, and take to the hills with me in the event of an invasion.

Being the youngest at Branksome Hilders I became a target for bullies. A dormitory fight broke out in my first week and the noise attracted the attention of the headmaster. 'What's going on?' he growled. 'It was Reeves,' they all chorused. He took me to his study and gave me a walloping. My eyes were full with the pain, but I had learned not to cry. No one likes a cry baby. When I returned to bed my leopard was missing. This small stuffed toy was precious. It had been with me for as long as I could remember. Thrown out of the window it was never found.

The headmaster Sidney Smith and his wife were *in loco parentis*, but parenting sixty small boys is impossible. Enforcing discipline and obedience - yes; care and attention to their needs - no. This upbringing instilled in me suspicion of father figures, even bishops with their croziers presenting themselves as caring Fathers in God, yet any misconduct and you get a walloping. But I anticipate.

Cubs and scouts were firmly on the school agenda. Sidney Smith and his wife were more frequently in scouts uniform than anything else, both bristling with badges, whistles and woggles. The high point of our scouting activities was the annual camp at Corfe Castle near Swanage. The scout master insisted that each morning the boys take off their pyjamas and roll in the dew, carefully avoiding cow pats and prickles. To embarrass us further a troop of girl guides some yards down the hill giggled at our mortification.

The war barely impinged on school life. Occasionally at morning prayers a notice would be given out about the war's progress. The headmaster officiated in a faded Oxford MA gown, green with age. The gown signified something important, but I never understood what. My first experience of religion - a hymn, a reading and some prayers - was intimidating. The headmaster had a plentiful supply of chalk which he regularly hurled at any boy who offended with some untoward noise. A pile of hymnbooks was at hand to deal with more serious disruptions.

Back home in Chichester life felt quite different. The peaceful cathedral city had become a sensitive military zone, the hub of a network of airfields including Tangmere and Thorney Island and airstrips at Westhampnett, Merstham and Selsey. The threat of invasion hung over the city for three years.

My mother managed her life and mine efficiently in the school holidays. We quickly got used to rationing, queuing and carrying identity cards. Gasmasks were issued to every household, but we never used them. Curtains had to be lined with heavy dark material to ensure complete 'blackout' at night. My father and various uncles built an air shelter, a 'dug-out', in the garden. When the air raid sirens blared we were supposed to leave the house and hide in the dug-out. We used the dank musty shelter once. With nowhere to sit and no light my mother declared: 'If we are going to die then we may as well die in comfort!' and we returned to the house.

The rise and fall of the warning air raid sirens were for me the scariest experiences of the war, also the racket of anti-aircraft gunfire trying to bring down German planes. The long steady note of the All Clear came as a relief. Most thrilling were the 'dogfights' between German and British planes high in the sky above Chichester.

I spent most evenings alone at home during the war. My mother needed to drive the car as a taxi and ambulance. I would wait up for her, my face pressed against the bedroom window. As soon as the car turned into the drive I climbed back into bed. My mother, sometimes alone, sometimes with an 'uncle', would look round the door, relieved to see me apparently asleep.

On 10th February 1943 a German bomber flew in low over the coast and made a daylight raid on Chichester. It completely destroyed my father's garage. At school, for an essay, I had to pretend to be a local journalist and wrote:

Mrs Reeves Saved by a Cigarette

On Tuesday at 2 o'clock a boy, one time worker of this establishment got into the garage. He put a lighted cigarette on an oil tin. He was going to steal some money. Then the siren started and an incendiary bomb fell on the place as well. Mrs

Reeves had gone to get a packet of cigarettes when the bomb started the fire. Everyone was killed except Mrs Reeves and the flames and bombs were going up and down like nine pins. The blaze was terrific and it was spreading to other shops and offices. Then suddenly 'whoooomph' a bomb fell and we were in blackness for a few minutes. The flames were quickly going and the smoke was thinner.

I was nine years old.

My mother determinedly carried on. Till the end of the war she ran the house, tried to keep the garden tidy, looked after me during the holidays and kept her taxi ambulance service going.

Occasionally we had company. My father had been married before meeting my mother. His first wife died while giving birth. Her sister used to visit during the holidays. Unmarried and the head teacher of a kindergarten in Newbury, Aunty May turned out to be the best company for a little boy. She laughed a lot; made a joke out of everything. She joined in my make-believe games, being a passenger on a double-decker bus while I pretended to be the conductor, and dutifully listening to my banging when I was given a small drum kit. At the age of twelve I used to play at churches. We put up a bell tent and I dressed in a sheet. She and my long-suffering black Persian cat made up the congregation and had to listen to my sermons that were always followed by a collection.

My holidays were mostly solitary. Strict rationing of petrol and lack of public transport made it difficult to meet children of my own age. I don't remember being particularly unhappy. I knew nothing different and lived a lot in my imagination.

Growing up I noticed we never talked about anything serious.

Life was all small talk. My father, a natural Conservative, read the *Telegraph* all his life. My mother had even less interest. She would have voted for Anthony Eden only because he was the best-looking man in politics.

We never talked about religion, which could not have been of less interest to my parents. When my father went to hospital and had to fill out a form he would answer questions about religion with a disparaging chuckle: 'Better put me down as Church of England.'

There were few books in the house. A set of Charles Dickens on the thinnest of Indian paper was a decoration. Eight years old, I tried to read *Nicholas Nickleby*, but I could make nothing of it. In fact my parents were voracious readers. Visits to Boots Library in Chichester became important weekly events. My mother preferred romantic fiction; she loved Daphne du Maurier, *Jamaica Inn* and *Rebecca*, Neville Shute and AJ Cronin. Meanwhile I devoured Enid Blyton, Percy F Westerman, WF Johns and later, all of Arthur Ransome.

These visits were part of my mother's routine. We walked the two miles into Chichester and then caught the 54 bus back home. I disliked shopping with her because she enjoyed meeting people and being celebrated for being the only survivor of the garage bombing meant engaging in endless conversations with every shopkeeper.

In the days before supermarkets, shopping constituted a social activity. As a treat my mother would take me to Fullers Restaurant for tea and walnut cream cake. One day, as a change, we went to the Dolphin and Anchor Hotel opposite the cathedral. I left my mother for a moment. Suddenly I heard her say: 'Come here at once!' more in embarrassment than anger. I had walked over to a white haired man dressed in black. I have often observed how timid but precocious children place themselves in front of a person whose attention they seek. I sat on his lap. The man was the Bishop of Chichester, George Bell: hence my mother's consternation.

For my tenth birthday I received a bicycle. This meant that I no longer had to endure shopping expeditions and could go where I wanted. There were limits to my explorations because throughout the war all the signposts had been removed and I easily lost my way.

One day I turned down a lane off the main road from Chichester to Petersfield and stopped outside a church, St Mary's Sennicotts, described by Pevsner as 'a sweet example of unselfconscious local nineteenth century Gothic'. Since my baptism I had never been in a church. I approached a large Gothic shaped door and pressed on a small brass knob. The door opened easily and I entered. My eyes led me to the east end of the church. Walking up the aisle into the sanctuary I observed the altar, a table covered by a cloth with a green frontal, and under it a collection of brooms, dusters and cleaning materials. I did not know the purpose of an altar but the clutter there did not seem right. Ever since when visiting churches I check what is hidden under the altar. Years later, the night before my induction at St James's Piccadilly, I looked beneath the altar and there they were: dusters, dustpans and brushes, brooms and a mop.

Rummaging round the church I came across a harmonium. Having recently begun taking piano lessons I could pick out hymn tunes. I visited St Mary's Sennicotts several times afterwards and felt at home in this little unpretentious church.

One day the door opened and a tall elderly priest came up to me at the harmonium. I felt scared but he immediately put me at ease. He seemed seriously interested in this ten-year-old boy. Nothing mattered but our conversation; he was reassuring, attentive and also respectful. No one had ever spoken to me like this before. He then left and I continued playing the harmonium. I often returned to the church hoping to see him again. The following summer holiday I discovered he had left. The priest I had met, Kenneth Latter, was an army chaplain who had won the MC and had stood in for the vicar, himself away as an army chaplain.

At thirteen I left Branksome Hilders and my parents sent me to Sherborne School, Dorset. Why Sherborne? According to my mother it was the furthest school away from home by rail, the Brighton to Plymouth line, which did not require a change of trains.

My father's return from the navy witnessed a deterioration in my parents' relationship.

He sat around the house all day in his dressing gown and did as little as possible. His perpetual laziness after the excitement of war exasperated my mother. When they began shouting I fled to my bedroom, feeling guilty and responsible.

Eventually my father bought a filling station in Lavant near Chichester. My mother regarded the new Reeves Garage as third best, but at least it kept him out of the house.

Though apprehensive about Sherborne I was relieved to be away from home.

In September 1947 my parents left me and my trunk on the pavement outside Abbey House, one of eight boarding houses in Sherborne School. The trunk had been carefully packed with uniforms for a twelve-week term, each item of clothing sewn by my mother with a name tag: D.St.J.Reeves.

I had reason to be fearful of what would happen to me here since this thriving replica of a nineteenth-century public school dedicated itself to honouring sport, cricket, hockey and mainly rugger above all else. We played rugger Mondays, Tuesdays, Wednesdays and Thursdays. On Fridays we dressed up in khaki and played at soldiers. Saturdays we had to watch and cheer the first or second fifteen playing a visiting school team. When bad weather made the playing fields too soggy we were sent on cross-country runs round the town. Boxing was compulsory for the first two years.

Rugger is reckoned to instil a number of virtues: the ability to inflict and absorb pain in equal measure; putting team spirit above the individual; breeding courage, comradeship, loyalty, endurance and self-discipline; an antidote to idleness and vice, generally meaning homosexuality.

At Branksome Hilders we played football haphazardly; at Sherborne, pitchforked into a game where the rules were never explained, I spent my years avoiding the ball, afraid of being hurt. The same went for cricket, positioning myself on the field as far away as possible from the wicket. On the one occasion I returned the ball to the wicket keeper I was mocked: 'Reeves, you throw like a girl!'

A couple of my contemporaries ran away. Some protested and were regarded as eccentric. I put up with this barbarism, permanently dreading the next day's two hours on the rugger field.

Sport contributed to Christian morality in the late nineteenth century, turning Sherborne into a model of muscular Christianity: physical fitness and manly character-building were partners in the age of advancing Christian imperialism.

Victorian educationalists valued 'manliness'. Sherborne had its own 'star' headmaster alongside Matthew Arnold of Rugby and

Edward Thring of Uppingham: the Revd Hugo Harper. He transformed Sherborne from a local grammar school with dilapidated and cramped buildings into a respected public school. A close friend of Edward Thring, the schools shared their joint hymnbook; Harper endorsed Thring's words: 'The whole efforts of a school ought to be directed to making boys manly, earnest and true.'

The Revd Frederick Westcott, unworldly, deaf and fanatical about rugger, glorified these notions of character-building. He made rugger compulsory at the school in 1893. He praised the victories of the First XV in his sermons. A contemporary recalls 'how the headmaster would roam about the touch line in clerical top hat and tails, a never-to-be-forgotten figure as he followed the game up and down, exhorting the school side in the quaintest of English, interspersed with expressions and quotations in Latin and Greek'.[1]

Forty years after Westcott, when I arrived in Sherborne, the values of sport and muscular Christianity still flourished. They needed no justification; they were part of the landscape.

Old Shirburnians returned to the school as teachers, keeping up traditions having known little else. Sherborne's isolation contributed to the ossification of tradition. 'That lonely Sherborne place', Dickens called it in 1856. A century later, John Betjeman described it as 'an Abbey town of golden ironstone, a town of schools'. Sherborne still feels isolated.

Alongside the idolatry of sport I had to endure fagging. A fag was a new boy who ran errands for house prefects. These duties included polishing shoes, making tea, coffee and toast, anything the prefect could not or would not do for himself. Public schools existed to train leaders to sustain and expand the empire; fagging familiarized boys with the dynamics of bossing and being bossed.

Discipline meant corporal punishment. Though headmaster and housemasters accepted this responsibility gladly most beatings were administered by the house prefects. Eventually promoted to house prefect I was warned to beat the new boys as hard as possible. It would not do for 'house spirit' to appear weak.

To be 'manly, earnest and true' meant suppression of emotions. Feelings could breed confusion, disruption and anarchy. Ancient Greek culture that so inspired Victorian headmasters with examples of sporting spirit and military prowess, also alerted them to the dangers of Dionysus, hence the constant exhortation to perpetual activity, preventing idleness and sublimating subversive sexual feelings.

This 'manliness' was achieved in the near complete absence of women. Women were necessary for cooking, cleaning, dusting, sewing and nursing – not suitable activities for boys striving to be manly. From the age of five when I went to Branksome Hilders until twenty, having completed two years of National Service, women were almost totally absent from my life.[2]

Occasionally at Sherborne our housemaster and his wife, he in a black tie, she in a long evening dress, invited senior boys to the 'private side' of the house. Gathering in the drawing room, crowded with chintz covered chairs and sofas, we drank sherry, listened to 78 rpm records, made friends with the golden Labrador and left as soon as we could.

Illness saved me from games, but when I caught measles the school had to be quarantined and this annoyed the First XV, whose away matches had to be cancelled. A kindly nurse transformed the sick room into a warm haven, a contrast to the rest of Abbey House, with its chilly draughty corridors, over-heated studies and doorless lavatories. Children sent away from home are considered to be in no need of care, but this I found in the sick room.

Girls were off limit. Anyone discovered setting up secret meetings would be expelled. My father once told me: 'Women are difficult. Don't have anything to do with them if you can help it!' My house-master in his birds and bees lecture to me added: 'Don't get married unless you have to!'

However, the annual Dance at Commemoration (to celebrate the gift of the School Charter) allowed boys to meet girls. I invited the sister of a friend and prepared for the pleasant but also terrifying prospect by taking ballroom lessons, paid for by Aunty May, and learned to foxtrot, quickstep, rumba and waltz with spin turns to the music of Victor Sylvester. I presented my partner with a box of chocolates. We were equally apprehensive. She had never danced before and I kept treading on her toes. She excused herself and after a while I went in a half-hearted search only to find her sitting happily with a group of other girls, scoffing the chocolates together.

My first experience of sex happened at Branksome Hilders where one of the masters used to see boys privately and touch us up. When he was caught and dismissed all of us were shocked only by the discovery that we had not been 'his special boy', as he used to tell each of us. At Sherborne boys masturbated; if together, then furtively in the dark. Sex had nothing to do with relationships. A teacher once berated a boy for being tired in class. 'Have you been masturbating?' 'Yes,' said the boy. 'When?' asked the teacher. 'Yesterday,' the boy replied. 'But that was Sunday!' exclaimed the teacher.

Rigid hierarchy made friendships between boys impossible. By the time I left the only boys I talked to were the other house prefects. The school discouraged friendships for fear they might undermine discipline. More fundamental reasons had to do with survival, manly independence and self-sufficiency. From the age of five I learned to survive by not trusting anyone. I only made friends within a group if it suited my survival. When no longer needed, those friends would be abandoned. Friendship became a game of emotional poker: always looking for the main chance.

Gradgrind's words from the opening pages of *Hard Times* could have been engraved over our classrooms: 'Now what I want is facts. Teach these boys and girls nothing but facts. Facts alone are wanted in life. You can only form the minds of reasoning animals upon facts and nothing else will ever be of any service to them.' Mediocrity of teaching added intellectual backwardness to emotional illiteracy.

Somehow I managed to secure a place at Queens' College, Cambridge on the strength of just two A-levels. However, my intellectual curiosity did not flower until I started studying theology ten years later.

At Sherborne my experience of religion centred on Chapel. The headmaster, Canon Alexander Ross Wallace, loomed large in dark robes and mortar board, the blackness relieved on Sundays by the white in his MA Cambridge hood. His voice rattled like a machine gun. In as far as I ever thought about what God looked like the headmaster came nearest to what I could imagine. I kept out of his way.

The Bishop of Sherborne confirmed me. A large man with a florid complexion his mouth remained open even when he did not speak and I spent the entire service staring at the bishop wondering what would happen if he swallowed a fly.

However, chapel became an important part of my school life but not for religious reasons. I learned the organ and sang in the choir, first as alto, then bass, my voice taking an alarming two years to break.

A minority of teachers began to break with tradition, recognizing there was more to life than building character through sport. When Ross Wallace left to become Dean of Exeter Cathedral a headmaster took over who was more enlightened. Sherborne today bears little relation to what I experienced in my first years there. However, the school continues to reinforce privilege, like all public schools.

I took to the organ readily. With little opportunity and no encouragement to practise, I never became as proficient as I would have liked. I played for Chapel services on Fridays; the console was in full view of the school. This was a novelty. People were impressed and my teacher even put me up for an organ scholarship at Cambridge. But I recognized the limits of my abilities. William McKie, the organist at Westminster Abbey, came to judge a musical competition at which I performed Bach's *Toccata and Fugue in D Minor*. He put his hand on my seventeen-year-old shoulder and said: 'Too much of you; not enough of Bach, young man!'

Each year we performed an oratorio in Sherborne Abbey. We sang Handel's *Messiah*, Bach's *B Minor Mass*, Haydn's *Creation*, Mendelssohn's *Elijah*, Brahms's *Requiem* and Elgar's *Dream of Gerontius* all at full throttle with organ and orchestra. For these occasions Robert Ferry, the director of music and conductor, wore morning dress. I enjoyed rehearsals. The attempts to synchronize organ and orchestra invariably turned into shouting matches between the conductor and Willie Wearden the organist. Wearden, red faced and with a broad Northern accent, liked to play his own way, and at his own speeds.

Along with being a musician I discovered I was also an actor. At home I went through a 'phase' (a favourite word of my mother's) playing at theatre with glove puppets. It came as a surprise to be asked to be Richard in Gordon Daviot's *Richard of Bordeaux*. I had already performed the part of the sickly sixteen-year-old Edward VI in *The Sherborne Story* and had to read out the Charter signifying that Sherborne was a King's school. But Richard of Bordeaux presented a greater challenge. The twenty-seven-year-old John Gielgud had just become a star in this play. Alec Guinness described him as 'having a fabulous voice like a silver trumpet muffled in silk'. At seventeen I had to play Richard from a young man to old age. Many lines perplexed me, not least the last words, when Richard speaks of his faithful friend: 'How Robert would have laughed.' To this day I do not know where the main accent should be.

As an actor I entered another world where I could release my imagination, to become another person. Music and drama helped me survive Sherborne.

On holiday I spent a lot of time alone, as usual, knowing no one my own age. Solitary life at Chichester was not disagreeable. Occasionally I helped my father at the garage. I enjoyed visiting my grandmother and aunts with my mother and continued reading my mother's library books, having outgrown the children's section at Boots Library. The complete works of Dickens remained unopened.

Then I discovered Chichester Cathedral.

The biggest building I had ever seen, my mother used it as a short cut between South and West Streets during our shopping expeditions in the war. After the war I visited the cathedral. It was then dark, dirty and shabby, heated by coal fired boilers; the acrid fumes filled the interior. I enjoyed the darkness and sat watching the few visitors, feeling completely safe and at home.

On one of my visits what seemed to me to be a very ancient, bald-headed clergyman greeted me. He invited me to tea. That is how I became a friend of Arthur Duncan Jones, Dean of Chichester. I visited the deanery regularly. The dean had eight children of his own, but I became one of a string of what were known in the Duncan Jones's family as 'daddy's young men' whom the dean took under his wing.

Only later did I learn that the dean presented a terrifying and forbidding figure. Either loved or loathed he had become a trenchant commentator on political and social issues. So when the Prime Minister Neville Chamberlain returned from his meeting with Herr Hitler at Munich in September 1938, and the majority of people greeted him with unqualified gratitude, Dean Duncan Jones sent telegrams to the Archbishops of Canterbury and York urging them 'to voice the conscience of England in protest against this most shameful betrayal in English history'. They ignored his telegrams.

At the time I knew nothing of these controversies. He gave his full attention to everything I had to say. His wife regularly served afternoon tea and cakes. Then the dean's verger would appear and help robe him for Evensong: first a cassock, then a long-sleeved surplice, then a tippet, then a black scarf, then academic bands, and finally a black skullcap. Led by the verger we walked slowly to the cathedral and I was shown to my seat next to the dean's stall. This became the pattern of our many meetings.

In 1955 during my time at Cambridge Arthur Duncan Jones died. I had visited him some weeks earlier. He sat propped up in bed, wearing his skull cap and gnawing a cooked chicken leg. He complained at not being able to attend the carol service.

I went regularly to the High Mass at the cathedral, captivated by the clouds of incense and thrilling improvisations by the organist, Horace Hawkins, who had been a pupil of the composer and organist Charles Widor. On special days trumpets supplemented the organ: an enthralling spectacle. I tried to share these experiences with my parents, who were unimpressed: 'just another phase'.

In September 1952 I started two years' conscription, National Service with the Royal Sussex Regiment where my public school background made me 'officer material'. Only medical grounds could have exempted me. At a cursory examination I had to drop my trousers, cough and be examined by a woman doctor, who passed me.

The first ten weeks I was incarcerated in the regimental headquarters in Chichester. For the first time I lived with men of my own age who came from 'the working class'. At Sherborne sex was never mentioned. Now no one talked of anything else. The men initiated me into a world of violent misogynistic attitudes to women with constant use of f and c words sharing sexual exploits remembered or anticipated. The women at the NAAFI must have had a hard time.

Male and hierarchical, Sherborne prepared me well for the army.

I made progress as a second lieutenant and was ready to leave the army two years later when Lt Colonel Ashworth, the Commanding Officer of the Royal Sussex Regiment, summoned me, suggesting the regiment make all arrangements to send me to Sandhurst and train as a professional if I wanted.

This was a tempting proposition as I felt at home in the army at the Assaye Barracks, Tidworth, base of the First Battalion. I led an easy, conventional, even lazy life. Weekends were free and I bought a half share in my first car, a 1929 Austin Swallow, known as *The Bullet*, for fifty pounds. I had also begun to develop my musical activities, conducting the regimental band at mess nights, learning the French horn and taking organ lessons with Douglas Guest, the organist at Salisbury Cathedral. My skills were put to the test when in 1954 the old colours of the Royal Sussex Regiment were ceremonially laid up in Chichester Cathedral. An elaborate series of mirrors were rigged up so I would be able to see the conductor from the console, high up in the organ loft. One of the mirrors broke and we only just managed to synchronize organ and regimental band in Vaughan Williams's arrangement of the Old Hundredth. I was also distracted by my mother whom I had invited to the service. She sat in the organ loft and spent most of the time peering over trying to catch the eye of Lancelot Mason, then Archdeacon of Chichester. Dressed in black with a broad brimmed hat, and accompanied by his black Labrador, his rugged good looks had caught my mother's attention on one of her shopping expeditions.

At Tidworth I contacted an attractive, warm-hearted and friendly girl whom I had met at the Three Choirs Festival in Hereford before starting National Service. She lived in the Close at Salisbury. After taking her out to dinner I accompanied her home and was about to say good night in the customary manner when I saw a curtain twitch, the front door then opened and her mother quickly pulled the girl inside. The mother glared at me and said: 'Oh, no you don't!' Then left me standing.

These diversions continued until the battalion moved to Minden as part of the British Army of Occupation of the Rhine. It had become less an army of occupation than one of defending West

Germany against the Soviet Union. As a platoon commander I left most of the work to the professional NCOs, the sergeants and corporals who regarded National Service officers with contempt: we were not the real thing. I had a batman who polished my boots and kept my uniform in good repair. General Sir Neville Mitchell of the Sixth Armoured Division appointed me acting ADC. My job was to liaise between the three brigades and divisional headquarters, carrying top secret documents from the general and attending briefing meetings. I commanded a light armoured car, the 'dingo', although there happened to be only a crew of one: the driver.

One day in a forest near Osnabruck the 'dingo' ran out of petrol. There were just the two of us, but I reared up pompously, swore at the driver and put him 'on a charge'. He said laconically: 'That won't help us, will it!' And we sat until help arrived.

This incident shows what an arrogant man I had become: just twenty years old, a prig and pleased with myself. 'You look like Rommel', I had been told after leading with sword drawn my platoon through Chichester at a ceremonial parade.

But I knew I would never be a professional army officer. A place at Queens' College, Cambridge, waited for me and there I went in 1954 to read English.

'Well,' said Uncle George while giving me a golf lesson, 'I expect you are putting the world to rights.'

My mother's brother, Uncle George, a farmer, was commenting on my being the first of my family to go to university. His curiosity had a trace of envy tinged with reproach: 'Isn't it time you did a proper job?' For my part I felt relief at leaving the army, and putting Sherborne and compulsory sport behind me.

I read English, the most popular degree course, appropriate for the many like myself who had no idea what they wanted to do with their lives.

Given the distractions of university life, I worked only intermittently, never finding enough time to read all the set texts. I found it easier to mug up Graham Hough on DH Lawrence, Theodore Redpath on the metaphysical poets, FR Leavis on George Eliot and Muriel Bradbrook on Shakesperian tragedy. I became adept at assimilating their insights and presenting them at tutorials.

FR Leavis had the most significant influence on me. He believed that nineteenth-century English literature in particular had a serious moral purpose in both its analysis and its cure. His entertaining lectures invariably began with a swipe at some reviewer in the *New Statesman*. Rude about his colleagues but attentive to his students, he believed that the study of literature should be a collaborative effort between teacher, student and the citizen. Whatever we commented on he would always say: 'Yes, but . . .' and make us look even more closely at the text.

FR Leavis was dismissed for his puritanical moralizing, his contempt for popular culture and his insistence that the modern world had destroyed what he considered a Golden Age. But I appreciated the high moral tone of his approach, one I was to recognize later in theologians who were to shape my life in the future.

I continued acting, taking small parts in at least one play a term. There were any number of theatrical companies of which the Bats of Queens' was one of the most flourishing. The Mummers, the Footlights and the Amateur Dramatic Club (ADC) were thriving. The people we talked about, noticed in the street and occasionally met at parties were to become celebrated actors and directors: Jonathan

Miller, Robert Chapman, Derek Jacobi, John Drummond, John Barton, David Frost and many others. But I was not single-minded enough to want to be a professional actor. I also lacked confidence in the company of these people.

I also accepted I would never become a cathedral organist. I took lessons first with the composer Peter Dickinson, Organ Scholar at Queens' College, who taught me how to phrase Bach's organ music, and later with George Guest, Director of Music at St John's College.[3]

Hesitantly my interest in religion began to develop.

I attended High Mass at Little St Mary's Church where the services reminded me of those at Chichester Cathedral. I sang in the choir at Queens' Chapel and occasionally played the organ for services. I also visited Monsignor Gilbey, the Catholic Chaplain at Fisher House. He kept his door open for everyone and disliked the telephone, keeping it in a cupboard.

In 1955, my second year at Cambridge, Mervyn Stockwood was appointed vicar of Great St Mary's, the University Church, which then rapidly became a fashionable venue among undergraduates. Mervyn Stockwood turned the church into a public forum. I joined the queue snaking down Kings Parade on a Sunday night to hear famous speakers including Stephen Spender, Fred Hoyle, Nye Bevan and Malcolm Muggeridge. They had been invited to comment specifically on significant contemporary issues such as the invasion of Suez in 1956, John Osborne's play *Look Back in Anger*, which was revolutionizing English theatre, and later the Wolfenden Report and burgeoning debates on nuclear weapons. Big questions were raised about which Mervyn Stockwood felt strongly, and St Mary's became famous as a centre of discourse and controversy.

Ten years later I became his chaplain and then in 1980 as Rector of St James's Piccadilly, inspired by his example I created another public forum – for London.

In those days, these and other clerics I met never gave the impression of wanting me to join their congregations. They were present and available for all of us students.

Henry Hart the Dean and Chaplain of Queens' College was a shining example of such a cleric. A life fellow of the college for sixty-eight years, lecturer in Hebrew and the Old Testament and owner of a large collection of Middle Eastern coins, he was formal, even severe. But he had deep affection for his students, knowing all of us by name. He invited me to join one of his reading groups, where we were allowed to read what we liked, so putting into practice Samuel Johnson's dictum that 'we should read from the first to last with utter negligence of all commentators', quoted by Henry Hart in his *Introduction to the Old Testament*. His other home was the Lake District and for years he invited students to undertake strenuous walks with him, taking off from the Rosthwaite Post Office guesthouse. His hospitality there and at Queens' became a point of sanity in my undergraduate life with its round of sleepless nights, drinking too much and doing all day and night what Uncle George described as 'putting the world to rights'.

If my experiences of the Church of England and the Catholic Church through Henry Hart and Monsignor Gilbey were largely benign, one incident made a significantly negative impression and left me angry and bitter for many years.

In 1956 the American evangelist Billy Graham led a University Mission from Great St Mary's. The prospect of this event filled the letter pages of *The Times*. As one correspondent put it, the invitation to Billy Graham 'raises an issue which does not seem to have been squarely faced. Universities exist for the advancement of learning. On what basis therefore can Fundamentalism claim a hearing at Cambridge?' I went to see what the fuss was about. Each evening meeting climaxed with an invitation to come forward and 'offer ourselves to Christ'. Curiosity made me walk up the aisle and kneel down. Asked if I wanted to 'accept Christ' I answered yes, gave my name and college, returned to my pew and thought no more of it.

The following day a member of the mission team asked to see me. For two hours he threatened, cajoled and bullied me to take Christ into my heart. Finally I gave in, knelt down by the ancient cracked leather sofa. He thanked the Lord triumphantly. Two days later I received a card from him congratulating me on my decision and telling me that on the bus back to Oxford he had prayed aloud for me. I felt abused, and replied asking him to remove me from his list. University had so far been stimulating and mind broadening; suddenly the threat of eternal damnation had turned the place into a prison. This experience cast a shadow over my life for many years.

While at Cambridge I began to loosen my ties with Chichester Cathedral, but not before getting to know the new dean there, Walter Hussey, a celebrated patron of the arts. He transformed the cathedral into a showcase for contemporary artists including Graham Sutherland, John Piper, Marc Chagall and Ceri Richards. He was very determined. When he commissioned Leonard Bernstein to write the *Chichester Psalms*, he told the composer: 'It is a little difficult to find the funds for this', to which Bernstein said: 'Yes, I know it is. These things are difficult.' Walter then said: 'Thank you for being so understanding.' And so the matter was dealt with. On another occasion, seeing a piece of work by Henry Moore, Walter told the sculptor: 'I really love this.' 'Oh, I am so glad you do.' 'Thank you very much,' said Walter, wrapping it up and taking it away. Describing himself as 'emphatically unmarried', he lived in the deanery with only his housekeeper for company. In contrast to his predecessor with his heavy furniture and book-lined walls, he preferred a Spartan, minimalist style. He enjoyed my company and for a time became my mentor.

Holidays were devoted to earning money, helping to pay my way through university and restore my bank balance. One year, for four months, Poly Tours employed me as a rep in San Remo, Italy. I had to chaperone young women more interested in meeting Italian boys than going on excursions I arranged. If there were not enough Italian men to go round I would be regularly woken in the middle of the night by Sandra or Stella, scratching at my bedroom door: 'We are having a party, come and join us!'

Showing off to two girls I had taken swimming in a cove surrounded by rocks, and diving into what seemed to be deep water but turned out to be shallow, I broke a bone in my neck. For two weeks I stayed in San Remo hospital, where the Italians made sure 'the *Inglese*' was never alone. My neck encased in a plastic collar, I collected a family of grandmothers and grandfathers who gathered every day around my bed, feeding me and teaching me Italian in exchange for English lessons.

By the end of my last year at Cambridge and still not sure what I wanted to do with my life, I visited the Cambridge University Appointments Board.

There were plenty of vacancies for arts graduates in advertising and industry so I had two interviews, one with the printing company De La Rue and another with J Walter Thompson, the advertising and marketing agency. Both assured me of the generous pensions I would receive in about forty years' time. I was not interested in these distant promises so I took an entry examination for the Foreign Office, but unable to answer questions on statistics, failed. The BBC also turned down my application to be a trainee graduate.

Eventually the British Council offered me a post, which I accepted, becoming one of eight graduates on a scheme to recruit men and women who would make the British Council a career. Initially they wanted to send me to Kyoto, but at the last minute changed my destination to Beirut: a sudden turn of events which would have important repercussions.

Beirut

The British Council offices in the 1950s stood in a smart fashionable district of Beirut near the American University. Once a villa, the offices still had the sense of a private residence. This became my work base for the next two years and the staff of five warmly welcomed me, curious about the fundamental changes to the organization I represented.

The British Council had been perceived until then as a refuge for dilettantes and eccentrics. A *Daily Mail* headline about the Council putting on a display of 'morris dancing in the streets of Cairo' during the invasion of Egypt in 1956 summed up this attitude. The Suez fiasco illustrated the humiliation of Britain as a world superpower, its imperial, political and military might being faced down. The British Council helped Britain's cultural influence flourish all over the world during these post-empire decades. And it continues to do so. Years later when I met Margaret Thatcher at a reception while she was prime minister, she and I discussed the merits of the British Council and for all our differences agreed on the vital importance of its work internationally. When I entered the service the organization needed overhauling and I belonged to the batch of new graduates who would launch the British Council as a branch of the civil service. We were the 'golden boys'. (There were no girls.)

Teaching English to a high standard from beginners to university level became our main task, mine in particular. The library and a busy programme of play-readings, exhibitions, lectures and debates were designed to promote the British way of life and culture in stimulating and even provocative ways and were meant to attract the Lebanese. However, audiences invariably turned out to be mostly English and American, such as at my first lecture on 'The Cult of the Dustbin', analysing new writing: John Osborne's *Look Back in Anger* and John Braine's *Room at the Top*.

I had just a week's briefing on how to teach English before leaving for Lebanon. We had to decide what method to use. Teaching English without translation became the only rule. With my limited French and non-existent Arabic, I knew no other way.

For all the radical changes in organization the British Council still used the old authorized textbooks: Eckersley's *Essential English for Foreign Students*. The books focused on the events in the lives of an insufferably conventional and boring middle-class English family from Purley: the Priestleys. Mr Priestley sat in his armchair pontificating while Mrs Priestley was forever getting out the tablecloth and laying the table. The family included a group of docile foreign students who happened to be living with them: Jan, Lucille, Olaf, Predrag, Frieda and Hob, all studying English via the Direct Method.

In spite of the Priestley family I quickly discovered my gifts as a natural teacher. I enjoyed teaching beginners as well as those fluent in English. No longer able to rely on the critical props of FR Leavis and company, I had to read the original texts and enjoyed doing this while introducing the Brontës, Henry James, George Eliot, DH Lawrence as well as Shakespeare to my students. My classes were oversubscribed and included, along with young students, diplomats, businesspeople and teachers.

I taught the Soviet ambassador for a time. A Soviet limousine would arrive every week to take me to the embassy. The steel doors opened and guards escorted me to the summer house where the ambassador waited, eager to learn about Charles Dickens and Robert Burns. Forty-five minutes later guards escorted me to the entrance and the limousine which drove me back to the office. These meetings took place during the Cold War, which was intensifying. After several weeks the meetings terminated abruptly. The ambassador had been recalled to Moscow in disgrace because of his pro-Western sympathies. I never found out what became of him.

One class differed from the others. I went regularly to the Officer Training School for the Lebanese Army. My class of more than forty cadets regarded these weekly lessons as an excuse to fool around (in the same way as I and my fellow soldiers did in Padre's Hour during training at Chichester Barracks). At first I arrived clutching copies of Eckersley's *Essential English* and realized immediately that the Priestley family held no interest whatever for these young men – all about my age.

I began with simple conversations, but the cadets were restless, looking for a chance to disrupt my flow. Once when I was explaining the difference between 'this' and 'that' one of the cadets stood up and exclaimed: 'Mr Revis, you are very beautiful!' Everyone laughed. Embarrassed, I then tried to explain what 'beautiful' meant.

The British Council may have decided to become more professional, and like everything else, would ultimately be market driven. But this development had not arrived yet and working life was relaxed. There were no targets to be delivered, no questions about impact.

My boss, Tom Moray, a former representative at the British Council's office in Baghdad, was easy going. Everyone got on well with each other, more or less.

Madam X, the receptionist and telephonist, sat at the hub of the office. A Russian in her fifties and carrying the weight of the world's suffering on her shoulders, she always looked about to burst into tears. Her favourite response to any question or observation was to shake her head from side to side sighing. At the telephone switchboard when too many demands were made on her she would remove all the plugs so no one could communicate internally or externally. For a moment she sat triumphant before resuming her customary morose gaze.

Those days such tantrums were tolerated.

I saw myself then as a buttoned-up, reserved, if garrulous Englishman. At Cambridge I planned my friendships with care, calculating the cachet of belonging to any particular group, a trait instilled in me during my years at Sherborne. In Beirut none of this seemed to matter. At the age of twenty-three my adolescence began.

These were the prosperous years of Lebanon before the catastrophe of civil war and the ravages of Middle East politics. Beirut had been independent from France for just ten years. It had become a confident, cosmopolitan, multi-ethnic, multi-faith, affluent city, a mix of East and West, of Muslim and Christian. Ottoman houses with red terracotta roofs stood next to Parisian-style nineteenth-century villas with high ceilings and arched windows. The city buzzed with restaurants, bars and nightclubs.

Many of my students were young women and I received a flow of invitations to go on 'picnic parties' to the beach, to Tyre and Sidon in the south and Byblos and Tripoli in the north. These occasions were exhausting because they provided my hosts with an excuse to practise their English. There were no romances. I had been brought up to believe that one day, out of the blue, I would fall in love and without rehearsal get married and carry on life as normal. These aspirations were reinforced by my mother's attachment to romantic fiction, so different from her own life, and the musicals of Ivor Novello with their happy endings.

I did form several deep friendships.

During summer, work in Beirut stopped at noon. Since there was no air-conditioning those who could afford it 'aestivated', which meant going up into the mountain villages to summer houses. A Jewish family welcomed me. A community of some two thousand Jews then lived in Beirut. Many of my students were Jewish. One of them, Moise Picciotto, scootered up into the hills with me on my Vespa to spend the afternoons and evenings at his family summer house sitting around with friends, playing pool, doing nothing much. I also made friends with Rheda, one of the few Muslims attending my class. Twenty years old he worked for the BBC and loved to walk. Some of my best memories of Lebanon were the walks we took together. The conversations were about everything and nothing, as is normal between friends. But when I left Lebanon in 1959 I never saw or heard from him again.

I also played the organ, giving two recitals including the first performance of *Meditation on Murder in the Cathedral* by Peter Dickinson, as well as Liszt's technically challenging *Prelude and Fugue on BACH*.

One day, while practising the organ accompaniment to Handel's *Messiah* in the hall of the American University where the concert would take place later, I had an unexpected encounter with Camille Chamoun, the President of Lebanon. My attempts at working out the pedalling for the 'Hallelujah Chorus' were interrupted by a cacophony of police sirens and screeching of breaks. A motorcade stopped outside. The president entered with a flourish only to discover he had arrived a week early for the concert. Though angry he acknowledged politely that it was not my fault.

I continued my passion for acting, playing the Soviet lead in Peter Ustinov's *Romanoff and Juliet*, a witty piece about a clandestine affair between two diplomats, mocking the steadily thickening crisis of the Cold War. The wife of an American diplomat played Juliet. It was some cheek to perform this particular play. The first night was attended by President Chamoun, the Soviet, American and British ambassadors, various religious leaders and assorted VIPs.

My career as a star actor ended there. The next time I appeared on stage was ten years later as the hind legs of a cow in *Dick Whittington*, the annual Christmas Pantomime at St Peter's Church, Morden.

The friendships I made in Beirut turned out to have important consequences for me.

I arrived in Beirut with a couple of suitcases, a portable gramophone and collection of 78s including Brahms's symphonies. Based in La Residence Hotel and looking for somewhere to live I met the third secretary of the British Embassy, Henry Carr.

Henry showed me Beirut and at weekends took me on expeditions around Lebanon. A popular, attractive and talented man (he trained to be a singer), interested in politics, and fan of *The Goons*, he was a diplomat with a bright future.

Since his flat stood within five minutes' walk of my office he invited me to move in with him.

Through Henry I met Kim Philby, the spy who was then Middle East correspondent for the *Observer*, and other journalists including Michael Adams from the *Guardian* and Peter Mansfield from *The Times*. They were all fiercely pro-Nasser, who represented resurgent Arab autonomy and independence from European imperialism. Through them I began to learn about politics in the Middle East. Kim Philby took a particular interest in my work with the British Council. He quizzed me about every aspect of my duties and I was only too happy to oblige, enjoying an audience. Years later when I learned about his being 'the third man' in the spy scandal involving Guy Burgess and Donald Maclean's defection to the Soviet Union, I could not reconcile the image of him as a traitor with the attentive and charming person who had been my friend.

Once I moved in with Henry our relationship deteriorated. He became possessive and I felt stifled just as I began to taste freedom for the first time. I had let myself in for something for which I was not prepared.

All this happened at a time of inner conflict. This struggle concerned religion. At that time I experienced religion as demonic, destructive and diminishing.

In my final year at Cambridge I had begun a journal, not a diary but notebooks in which I wrote privately how I felt about God. Fifty years later it is shocking to read these jottings because the God I then endeavoured to worship was God the Father, stern, merciless and unforgiving.

The only way I thought I could please this God was to pray more, meditate more, read the Bible more. In Beirut, even as I began to enjoy my freedom, I created a punishing apparatus of spiritual practices. If I chose to do too little, then clearly I could not be praying hard enough, so I had to do more. If I set myself impossible targets, like meditating for an hour as soon as I woke up, then I was certainly not good enough and had to try harder. I put myself in a no-win situation.

The spiritual battles in Cambridge were about the important issue of what I should be doing with my life. Ordination was then not on the agenda. In Beirut the questions of ordination began to appear, but these questions were really about my acceptability to God. I must do this, do that. 'Must' appears constantly in these jottings. Behind them lay unresolved questions, about my sexuality, about harnessing my creativity, about who I was.

The demonic, destructive and diminishing nature of this God represented forces from which I could not escape. Often at breaking point these forces constantly threatened my creativity as a teacher and a musician.

Even fifty years on, it remains a mystery where this tyrant God came from. Certainly not from my own father; perhaps from my encounter with the Billy Graham Mission at Cambridge; perhaps from an accumulation of repressed desire, guilt and duty brought forward from Sherborne.

I gravitated to the Anglican Church of All Saints in Beirut. The affable but vague and distant priest did not want to have anything to do with me. There were rumours he had a drink problem. An unspoken rule declared that Sunday Service, Matins, should be over within an hour so the congregation would not be late for cocktail parties. On special days the British Ambassador read the second lesson. Women always wore hats. As part of my self-imposed penance I once read St Mark's Gospel at one sitting. Its radical demands and threats made me fearful to read more of the Bible. For a time I tried reading a few verses a day from the Bible Reading Fellowship, but I lost interest.

What I appreciated most about All Saints was the Anglo-American Club next door. Here with its signed photographs of President Eisenhower and of the young Queen Elizabeth II I could chose from an English menu and use the swimming facilities.

Along with 'must' the word 'stranded' appears frequently in these jottings. I lived two lives like two clashing themes in a Charles Ives symphony. Stranded with the struggle to do better I felt alone, without spiritual companionship. Occasionally I would argue with my British Council colleagues. Being seasoned agnostics they invariably trounced my arguments and then I would write in my notebook: 'I must be a faithful apologist' – another 'must'.

But at the same time I discovered a gift for being sociable and gregarious.

A third and more hopeful dimension eventually and slowly emerged out of a period of great stress.

In 1958 came the first murmurings of the troubles and civil wars which have all but destroyed Lebanon. The aggressively pro-Western President Camille Chamoun came into conflict with those Arab countries which had broken off relations with Britain after the invasion of Suez. Chamoun refused to join them. Prime Minister Rashid Karami, a Shia Muslim, and Walid Jumblatt, leader of the Druze community, were determined not to allow the president the last word.

President Chamoun asked for assistance from the American Sixth Fleet and army to secure the airport and the port of Beirut.

Some of us went to watch the disembarking of the troops on the beaches of Beirut. Dressed in full body armour and bristling with ammunition, the soldiers weaved their way between bikini clad sunbathers and ice cream vendors.

A nightly curfew sealed the success of the invasion. Anyone on the streets after 7.00pm could be shot.

Cooped up in the flat with Henry I became anxious about his mood swings. Occasionally we would be invited to pyjama parties: 'Bring your pyjamas, have dinner, and stay the night.' But most nights we were alone together.

To calm my nerves I attended Mass at an ugly modern Franciscan Church every morning before going to work. I usually arrived at the end of Mass as the lights were being switched off. I sat at the back in the dark like I used to do in Chichester Cathedral as a small boy, and caught my breath. I sat still. I did not kick-start the engine of my religious rigmarole. I sat. I breathed quietly and consciously, living in the moment, preparing myself for the day ahead.

Over the days I received what I can only describe as a gift, not mediated by anyone or anything. The gift came with the words 'Do not fear; you will be all right.'

Years later in a sermon by Paul Tillich, in *The Shaking of the Foundations*, I recognized what I experienced in that Beirut church:

We cannot transform our lives, unless we allow them to be transformed by a stroke of grace. It happens; or it does not happen ... Grace strikes us when we are in great pain and restlessness. It strikes us when we walk through the dark valley of a meaningless and empty life ... It strikes us when the longed-for perfection of life does not appear, when the old compulsions reign within us as they have for decades, when despair destroys all joy and courage. Sometimes at that moment a wave of light breaks into our darkness, and it is as though a voice were saying: 'You are accepted, *you are accepted*, accepted by that which is greater than you, and the name of which you do not know. Do not ask for the name now; perhaps you will find it later. Do not try to do anything now; perhaps later you will do much. Do not seek for anything; do not perform anything; do not intend anything. *Simply accept the fact that you are accepted!*' If that happens to us, we experience grace. After such an experience we may not be better than before, and we may not believe more than before. But everything is transformed.[4]

Theologians and preachers sometimes say far too much. I was not transformed then and there, but I recognized enough in Tillich's words which resonated in my own life.

Atheists irritated by this "emotional waffle" say: 'You were just exhausted and wanted a break.' To which I respond: 'You are right, but why reduce everything to *just*? Can't you understand the depth and width of what I am describing?'

They say: 'Why can't we have this experience, then?' And I respond: 'I do not know.'

At which point the conversation falters.

After my experience in the Franciscan Church in Beirut I did not emerge in a glow of cosmic love. But I glimpsed in that church another way, altogether more hopeful.

Yet the tyrant God in his demonic, destructive and diminishing way returned to haunt me so I decided I should be ordained. The only way out was to hand myself over to God, all of me. I did not know how people would react to my decision; but I was now angry with God. 'Sod it,' I said. 'Here I am.'

On leave in 1958 I went on a retreat to Stacklands Retreat House and wrote in my book: 'I must do whatever God wants', and later: 'I will meet God; merely listen; and do what I'm told.'

In this mood of resentment and confusion I presented myself as a candidate for ordination to the Bishop of Chichester, Roger Wilson. I met him again forty years later at Mervyn Stockwood's funeral. Roger Wilson, now ninety years old, on seeing me exclaimed: 'Ah! I remember you. You were a special case and I have followed your career with great interest!'

Following his recommendation I attended a selection conference, much on the lines of the War Office Selection Board (a Board for selecting officers). I passed and went to visit Cuddesdon Theological College.

It was the only theological college I had ever heard of. I spent twenty four hours there. When I left, I said to myself: 'If that's Christianity, give me measles!'

I found the atmosphere earnest and dull. The students told me that the principal lived on onion soup and that he preached frequently on death, especially at Easter. Edward Knapp Fisher, the principal, had a reputation as a sympathetic pastor. The day I saw him he was dour, reserved and withdrawn to the extent we could not have a conversation.

I was offered a place in 1959.

But then I decided not to go to Cuddesdon.

Realizing that I knew nothing about the Church of England I tried to discover what a vicar did. What did he do on Mondays?

Soon I realized I had no interest whatever in the answers to those questions.

In my notebooks I wrote: 'There is a great temptation to throw up all this religion.' The sentence was heavily underlined.

I followed this piece of advice to myself, putting religious rigmarole to one side. But old habits die hard and when it came to leaving Lebanon in 1959 I found myself caught up in the same battles I could not win, although they had become less intense.

Then convinced that I was the only person in the world to experience these sorts of struggles I would discover they are commonplace, especially in my experience working in Central London thirty years later. Faced with declining numbers many clergy do all they can to rope people into church. At St James's Piccadilly I advised many to stay away from religion until they had begun to grow up.

Meanwhile having made an important decision to leave religion behind, I carried on with my work in Lebanon and awaited the news of the next posting in the British Council with eager anticipation.

Phonemes

Relieved at my decision not to accept the offer of a place at Cuddesdon Theological College I returned to Beirut. Henry had been transferred to London pending his appointment as the Cultural Attaché at the British Embassy in Brussels. We lost contact and never met again. Many years later I came across a news item tucked in the middle of a newspaper reporting his death, murdered in his Notting Hill flat by a rent boy.

I moved into a small flat of my own. Politically Lebanon returned superficially to normality. The American Marines left. The extreme pro-Western President Camille Chamoun had been replaced by a moderate Maronite, General Chehab.

I attended All Saints Church occasionally and stopped beating myself up. The number of 'musts' declined. But it took many years before my image of God as the stern father faded. As the writer Tom Wolfe says: 'You never realize how much of your background is sewn into the lining of your clothes.'

Work kept me busy. In September 1958 the Ministry of Education in Jordan together with the British Council held a summer school for seventy secondary school teachers of English at Ramallah; its aim was to learn about classroom development of language skills. But I had to lecture on Goldsmith, Keats, Wordsworth, Tennyson, Lewis Carroll and Shakespeare's poetry. Each session lasted three hours. I also gave an introduction to the films of Dickens's *Great Expectations* as well as Oscar Wilde's *The Importance of Being Earnest*. The Jordanese teachers spoke English to an average standard but none of them had visited England or knew much about English literature.

My year's experience in Beirut teaching to university level, aware of being an amateur in the tradition of Christopher Isherwood in pre-war Berlin, had made me thoughtful about guiding students into a foreign culture. I considered my task to lead students into a foreign land where they could begin to absorb the culture, sensibilities and assumptions, before returning to their own world. I knew instinctively to hold on to the 'strangeness' of the world of William Wordsworth, not explaining away, or modernizing or making hasty value judgements. 'This is how it was,' I would say. 'Now stay with it.'

Of course, weighty questions began to surface; in particular how does, how should the past, its culture and history, relate to the present? This movement between cultures, passing from one to another then returning to the world today, is a lifetime's work. Later at St James's Piccadilly when I preached from the Bible and gave expositions at Bible seminars, I tried to move backwards and forwards, holding a constant dialogue within myself and also with the congregation. Back and forth: this dialogue often illuminated parts of a landscape long obscure.

From FR Leavis and years later from the Old Testament scholar Walter Brueggemann I learned the paramount importance of staying close to the text. In 'Criticism and Philosophy' in *The Common Pursuit*, Leavis writes that the reader should:

realize as sensitively and completely as possible this or that which claims his attention. He must be on his guard against abstracting improperly from what is there in front of him, and against any premature or irrelevant gazing – of it or from it. His first concern is to enter into possession of the given poem in its concrete fullness and his constant concern is never to lose his completeness of possession but rather to increase it.[5]

So, in Ramallah, we considered, for example, Wordsworth's 'Daffodils'. No one had ever seen a daffodil there and, this being long before the days of PowerPoint presentations, I did not even have a photograph. Eventually one was found. I tried to explain the English Romantic poet's view of nature, and the particular fascination of the Lake District – not to explain it away, but to present it. Then we read the poem. We had to work on the text: words like *vales, margin, sprightly, jocund* and *inward eye*. They needed elucidation. Then back to the text, to the end of the poem: 'the bliss of solitude and then my heart with pleasure fills/And dances with the daffodils'. How is it possible for daffodils to create so much joy, so much elation? Then I asked about their attitude to their own environment, the mountains, hills, desert and water of Jordan.

The Ramallah Conference could not happen today. The highpoint was a picnic in Bethlehem.

In June 1959 I had hoped for a posting to Kyoto where the writer and critic Professor DJ Enright lectured, but was instead recalled to London to study for a certificate in Linguistics at the Institute of Education.

I packed my bags and left Beirut.

Of all the places I have lived and worked Lebanon evokes the deepest melancholy. I am reminded of how transient our experience is: here today, gone tomorrow – so little to show for it.

Lebanon imploded in the long civil war that began in 1975 and Israel's bombardment destroyed most of the country's surviving infrastructure in 2006. Beirut has changed beyond all recognition. Today the Islamification of Lebanon is unstoppable.

The root cause of the country's collapse is Lebanon and the West's failure to sufficiently recognize and respect Muslims. In the 1950s Muslims were generally ignored, regarded as second-class citizens. An Armenian Catholic family attended lectures at the British Council. They lived in a district overlooking the Sabra and Shatila camps, full of Palestinians driven out of Israel. 'They are refugees,' the family said. 'We can see the camps from the balcony of our apartment. Now we are moving. We do not want to be reminded.'

Friends died in the civil war. Others, Maronite Christians, left for France or the USA. The destruction of Beirut is a graphic reminder of the fragility of cosmopolitan cultures.

Intangibles sharpen the poignancy of the transience of our experience. In spite of my inner religious turmoil I had begun to grow and live in Lebanon, expending constant effort on making music, acting, teaching and lecturing, meeting all sorts of people, engaging in long discussions. Places recall these encounters and activities: walking by the Litani River in South Lebanon on warm evenings (the Litani is now under Israeli control); searching for the source of the Adonis River in the silence of the mountains; lively conversations at the Lucullus Restaurant and along the Corniche in Beirut; skiing near Tripoli, among the cedars of Lebanon where an altercation with a cedar once resulted in a twisted ankle; enjoying cool summer evenings in Faluja in the mountains above Beirut.

I was a privileged well-paid foreigner playing a minor part in international cultural 'manifestations' (as the French called them): entertainments, some brash and pompous, others like the Baalbek Festival, supported by the British government through the British Council, which in its heyday then had the reputation of being among the best international arts festivals in the world. All that energy expended; creativity wiped out.

Back in London I enrolled as a student at the Institute of Education.

The British Council invested money in developing my professional skills. In Beirut the British Council paid for me to learn Arabic. I took a nine-month course of lessons with Mr Hitti. Round, bald and always wearing a grey suit, grey shirt and grey tie, Mr Hitti's teaching methods would not have been approved by Mr Eckersley. He began lessons practising his English, rehearsing aphorisms he had learned such as: 'Life without a wife is like a kitchen without a knife', referring obliquely to my bachelor status. His body would shake as he laughed at his own jokes.

Only then did the lesson begin. After nine months I could write and speak Arabic. Mr Hitti presented me with an Arab daily newspaper. I read it aloud and he corrected me. But I had no idea what it meant. 'Translation is the next stage,' he would say. The lessons came to an end before we reached that point and I forgot Arabic soon after.

Dr William Lee, who had organized the conference for teachers at Ramallah, observed my ignorance about linguistics. Some months later when I joined a small team in Reykjavik in Iceland he listened to my lectures on modern English Literature, which confirmed his suspicions about my ignorance. He told the British Council to send me to the Institute of Education.

Dr Lee was a pioneer. He single-handedly transformed the teaching of English as a foreign language from the preserve of the amateur into a professionally equipped teaching force.

But I had no interest in linguistics, only in literature. After an interminable tutorial on phonemes I resigned.

Meanwhile I had been offered a job as Director of Studies at Brasted Pre-Theological College. I accepted and in January 1959 left the British Council and started a new life.

On the Way to Ordination

Christopher Martin, editor of *Prism*, had recommended me for Brasted. He and his friend Robin Minney founded the magazine. Recently graduated from Oxford, both were bright, educated and thoughtful. Christopher Martin, a tax inspector, and Robin Minney, a teacher, established *Prism* for graduates and professional people of their own generation. Its aim was to make membership of the Anglican Church more than nominal. I came across *Prism* accidentally in London, and gladly paid my one shilling a month subscription, which after six months rose to one shilling and sixpence.

Prism was unlike anything else I had come across in reading about religion.

The freshness and directness of the contributions in *Prism* appealed. Nicholas Mosley, the novelist who later became one of the editors, wrote:

> One of the things which the magazine has got to do is to try desperately to avoid church language and to base its appeal on what could be called good writing in the literary or journalistic sense. I realize good has no absolute value; it is just a taste, but there it is, and it is what sells articles in the modern market.

Church language is often embarrassing. So much theology and preaching gets stuck in abstractions: love, forgiveness, redemption, salvation. Abstractions shrivel the soul. Even today when I sit in a congregation listening to an overworked or lazy bishop or priest droning on I want to interrupt and say: 'Shut up, get real! What are you talking about?'

Prism asked the question: What is wrong with the Church of England? Why is it so gutless? The answer came: Because it is an establishment Church. Disestablishment became one of the recurrent themes in *Prism* alongside nuclear disarmament, race relations, education, the abolition of the death penalty and issues around sex. Austin Farrer, the Anglo-Catholic Oxford theologian and one of the most luminous preachers of the day, wrote on prayer.

Robin Deniston, publisher and author, reflecting on three years of *Prism*, got the tone right when he wrote: 'With many high hopes and intentions to provide bridges over gaps, comprehensible devotion for girl friends, forums for this and that.'

Prism never attracted more than five thousand readers and it became incorporated into *New Christian* in 1965. *Prism* and *New Christian* have been described as a 'radical's lonely hearts club'.[6]

Prism became the catalyst for me to start reading theology seriously. It provided an intellectual stimulus which became an important reason why I did not give up on ordination.

Archbishop Michael Ramsey once told me of his reading addiction: 'I read often and in secret.' I know what he meant. I have also read theology widely and promiscuously ever since those early months of *Prism* in the late 1950s.

I had written to Christopher Martin from Beirut about *Prism* and he suggested a meeting. About to leave Brasted to become the Independent Broadcasting Authority's watchdog on religious programmes, he proposed me as his successor.

Brasted Place was a country house built by the Georgian architect Robert Adam for George III's physician. It was purchased by Napoleon III, who from there prepared for his disastrous invasion of Boulogne. Locals described him parading up and down the main road between Westerham and Sevenoaks with his tame eagle in attendance.

In 1952 an Anglican priest, David Stewart Smith, and his wife Kathleen bought Brasted Place. They aimed to establish a residential college for those who wished to be ordained but who had missed out on the traditional route to ordination: public school and university. This initiative, alongside others such as Rochester

Theological College for men over forty, was in response to considerable anxiety about the rapid decline of ordinands for the Church of England.

The two-year course at Brasted helped students resume their education and then, as the prospectus put it: 'supply a general background of intelligent study and thinking which is needed before theological training can profitably begin'.

Three resident staff members, the warden, the chaplain and the director of studies, provided the two-year course. My responsibility was primarily for the first-year course. I gave a series of lectures and seminars on the history of ideas, including an elementary course on philosophy and logic. I repeated and expanded my work on English literature, taught nineteenth-century history and shorter courses on ethics and civics.

The favourable conditions at Brasted made this considerable workload possible. I was free to develop and change the courses. The staff–student ratio was one to nine.

In 1961 the Church Advisory Council for Training for the Ministry sent two assessors to report on the college (one of them, John Brewis, was one of my predecessors at St James's Piccadilly). This was an important moment for the Stewart Smiths, since the report would officially endorse the college's work. We passed with flying colours.

The report described me as 'having a stimulating mind, friendly and provocative both in the lecture room and outside'. They noted how I began every session by reading a poem and that my rooms resembled an Oxbridge College. They described Brasted as a 'mellow well lived in country house'.

The assessors likened Brasted to a tiny university college, observing how the students were encouraged to develop their capacity to think and talk on their feet and 'continued discussions on walks and in bed sitting rooms in the best university tradition'. In fact most of us went regularly to the White Hart at the bottom of the drive for a beer.

The college felt like an extended family. Kathleen Stewart Smith, a formidable woman, acted as domestic bursar, housekeeper and stand-in cook. When a visiting bishop came for supper and asked how many children she had, she replied without blinking: 'Twenty eight'.

The college functioned as a traditional theological college with a compulsory but relaxed timetable of simple formal worship which I took part in – sometimes most reluctantly.

Brasted closed in 1974 for lack of funds.

At the end of my first year four students and I bought a 1928 Chevrolet and drove to Jerusalem. This adventure tested our relationships. The car had no air-conditioning; the heat became often intolerable. Once a student strode off into the desert between Istanbul and Ankara, complaining how another made him 'very angry'.

In Jerusalem I was given permission to play the organ at the Church of the Holy Sepulchre once the Greek Orthodox and Armenians had been consulted. The organ was spread out in the rotunda above the sepulchre. With no sheet music I improvised messily on 'Praise my Soul the King of Heaven'. Just as I got into my stride a Franciscan arrived and agitatedly shooshed me. I had to stop because a service was about to begin.

We returned via Beirut. We met two of my old friends, former students, and I wished we had not gone to Beirut. We were just tourists there. My companions in the Chevrolet did not know, because I could not tell them, that I had left my heart in Beirut.

Teaching ordinands and beginning to discover some intellectual curiosity about theology in *Prism*, on my return I decided to revisit Cuddesdon.

Robert Runcie was the new Principal. I immediately warmed to his inner modesty.

Cuddesdon had become less earnest, more relaxed. I could fit in and in 1962 I became a student for four terms, provided I could pass some of the general ordination exams. I took these at Brasted, sitting for five papers with the students I happened to be teaching in their second year, passed and completed the rest at Cuddesdon.

My decision to return to Cuddesdon came with considerable misgivings. I could not see myself as a priest, having to relinquish teaching that I loved. I also felt I might be deceiving the Church of England. My dissembling arose from the difficulties I had in inhabiting the church structures. This is where *Prism* and *New Christian* opened doors for me: sustaining and encouraging my enquiries. I developed an ambivalence about religion, Christianity and the Church of England which has never left me.

At Cuddesdon decisions had to be made as to where I would fetch up as a curate; I was content to go wherever I was sent. There were jobs all over England and at that time enough money to pay us. Robert suggested Maidstone Parish Church.

I arrived at the vicarage determined to be on my best behaviour. Neil Nye, the vicar, greeted me warmly, announcing: 'We are just making angel wings for the nativity play; here's the wood, the plastic, scissors and glue. See how you get on!'

The vicarage was open house. I met most of the church council and the church wardens, one of whom said: 'If you come here, we'll soon lick you into shape!' Neil invited me to join the staff of two priests and two deaconesses. I accepted. On Trinity Sunday 1963 Archbishop Michael Ramsey ordained me deacon in Canterbury Cathedral.

As we assembled for the procession, I overheard the archbishop's chaplain, John Andrews say to the archbishop: 'Your Grace, this is a special day. There are trumpets!'

'Ah!' said Michael Ramsey beaming, 'Yes, yes, yes!'

Apprentice

The year of my ordination, 1963, saw the publication of John Robinson's *Honest to God*. But the 1960s had not yet arrived at All Saints Maidstone.

Built in 1395 the church has been described as the widest Gothic Perpendicular church in England. Dusty regimental flags, the colours from the Royal West Kent Regiment, hung from the ceiling in the side aisles. Twenty-four misericords for the college of priests, founded in the fifteenth century, stand in the choir stalls. A heavy Victorian screen then divided the chancel from the nave.

The church is both a parish church and a civic church, serving the borough and county of Kent. My vicar, Neil Nye, was a gentle and generous priest. He presided over a thriving congregation, mainly middle aged, middle class, prosperous, confident and conservative.

When Archbishop Geoffrey Fisher retired in 1961 declaring: 'I leave the Church of England in good heart', he could have had one of his most prominent parishes All Saints Maidstone in mind.

Geoffrey Fisher's primacy is remembered as a time of prudent housekeeping, reconstructing the Church of England's finances to ensure decent clergy salaries, repairing churches damaged in the war, building churches for the widespread housing estate programme set up by Prime Minister Harold Macmillan. Though opposed to the Suez invasion Geoffrey Fisher was conservative, Protestant and Establishment to his fingertips. As a former headmaster he could not resist the habit of reprimanding bishops or peers in the House of Lords when he disagreed with them.

I met him just once during my time at Brasted. He arrived for a preaching engagement and I opened his car door to greet him, finding him sound asleep with spectacles propped on his forehead. 'Where am I?' he asked on waking. He roused himself quickly, preached a brisk sermon and left. He was the last bishop to wear breeches, gaiters, frock coat and apron, the traditional uniform when bishops rode round their dioceses in the eighteenth century. He took advantage of his position as archbishop to order bishops to continue dressing like this, but several, including my future boss Mervyn Stockwood, refused. On becoming the next archbishop Michael Ramsey dropped the tradition, preferring suit or cassock.[7]

The only innovation at All Saints at that time was the gradual replacement of Choral Matins as the principal service on a Sunday by Parish Communion. Discussions went on for many months on how and where the Eucharist should be celebrated, and unlike in many other churches, the debates were managed sensitively and without rancour. All Saints removed the Victorian screen after I left, something I supported enthusiastically at the time, though the interior looks even more cavernous without it.

We described ourselves as 'the church family', or 'the family of the church'. But we represented a family of the most traditional kind. Divorced couples, single parents and gay people were not welcome. People within this conservative congregation behaved with kindness to one other, but the undeclared policy remained: 'No change'.

'Family' meant opportunities had to be created for members to meet outside worship. The church organized many social events; a highlight of the year was the parish holiday.

Neil Nye's previous parishes, first at Clapham then the St Helier Estate in Morden (where I would also be vicar later), both in South London, made him realize that for many workers two weeks' holiday in a healthy environment, by the sea, was beyond their means in the years immediately following the war. However, my job with Poly Tours in the mid-1950s already indicated how increasing affluence in the working classes made package holidays popular. The wet sands and unreliable weather of Blackpool would soon give way to the guaranteed sun on the Costa Brava.

Nevertheless, Neil Nye continued the tradition of the parish holiday. For two weeks in August the church 'family' took over a prep school in Stockbridge. Each day started with prayers and Bible study. Then the fun began: trips to the seaside, picnics, hide and seek, treasure hunts (for which I laid the trails), and if it rained, party games and sardines. Evenings were devoted to singsongs and opportunities for the clergy to make fools of themselves – to show they were human like everyone else. The vicar, his two curates and two deaconesses acted like redcoats at a Butlins Holiday Camp.

This reminded me of a holiday job during my last year at Cambridge. Six of us worked at the Butlins camp in Skegness, where the motto was: 'Our true intent is all for your delight'. The redcoats comprised the entertainment staff, who made sure, even compelling the holiday campers to have a jolly time. I chose to work in the kitchen, where one of my friends, the novelist David Rees, was sacked for calling a particularly difficult holiday camper 'a bloody peasant'. The rest of us organized a strike among the other students working there and brought the camp to a halt for several hours, after which we were dismissed as well.

Now I had become a religious redcoat.

Because of a shortage of adult chairs at Stockbridge we had to sit on low benches or perch uncomfortably on children's stools. Two weeks of Stockbridge resembled a constant office party without drink or sex.

Though a few families came on the parish holiday, most of the people there were single, female and in their fifties. Some were spinsters; others had lost husbands in the war.

I found the role of religious redcoat irksome. I had not reckoned on the effect of the clerical collar. A priest was expected to be perpetually available and amiable. Being nice meant small talk. Never adept at this I had to grow into the kind of cleric who, with a slight stoop, shows immense concern over whatever is being talked at him, the day's weather or just nonsense. In many cases, including my own, this appearance of concern provided a way of concealing boredom, inadequacy and shyness. However, the skill of being programmed to please can turn this availability into a spiritually draining treadmill.

Clergy often infantilize adults. The benches and children's chairs at Stockbridge were symptomatic of more than a shortage of proper seating arrangements. Men in the congregation mostly held positions of authority: church wardens, treasurers, members of finance committees. In this way they made themselves indispensable.

Clergy were not only expected to be nice, but also we must not rock the boat. As a teacher I had always spoken my mind freely, useful in getting students to learn. Now I had to deal with silencing and censorship.

Therefore sermons failed to connect with the congregation, because I felt the church inhibited me from being specific. 'Love in Action', the first of over two thousand sermons I have ever preached, ended like this:

As we grow in the understanding and awareness of the needs of others, so we shall be loving God and experience something of his love for us. Amen.

But I never identified who these 'others' might be. I wanted to say they were those most unlike us, those who do not fit in, those who upset us. I needed to name them.

Despite these strictures I appreciated learning the craft of priesthood at Maidstone: officiating at baptisms, weddings and funerals and handling all the sensitive personal contact these entailed.

I was more myself in my church role as teacher to the sixth forms at Maidstone Grammar School. None of these students came to church, but they enjoyed the opportunity of meeting to discuss important issues. Occasionally I spoke at assembly and would choose a lyric from the Beatles, interpreting it in some spiritual or Christian way. FR Leavis would have turned in his grave.

Ann Kerr, the MP for Rochester, inspired me to join the Campaign for Nuclear Disarmament, founded in 1958. I attended meetings and rallies with anyone I could persuade to accompany me. CND, a grave, serious and simple cause, was then a movement of dissent. We believed naïvely and mistakenly that our moral fervour would influence the Kremlin and Washington.

Two events at All Saints Maidstone gave warning of the kind of priest I would become, precursors of the future.

First, I preached a sermon at the Assize Service. Then I wrote and produced a nativity play.

They both touched raw nerves and stirred up controversy and subsequent uproar which, not having experienced anything like this before, I was not yet ready to handle.

All Saints took civic religion seriously. In the 1950s the Establishment governed every part of society and expected the Church of England to conform and not confront. The Coronation in 1953 affirmed the nation's Christian values. Patriotism, duty and deference were celebrated and Britain experienced a renewed sense of identity after the disruption of war and the collapse of empire. As a second lieutenant I hitchhiked up to London from Tidworth with some friends and stood in the pouring rain for many hours, cheering both the news of the conquest of Everest and the arrival of a smiling Queen Salote of Tonga riding in an open carriage without umbrella. She waved back at us. The biggest cheer went up for the London County Council street cleaners clearing up after the horses.

The same values expressed at the Coronation operated locally at civic occasions, in particular the Assize Service, the most significant annual service in the county of Kent. Politicians, mayor and town council attended along with judges in their wigs and ermine. Neil Nye asked me to preach the sermon and I chose a text from the Book of Amos: 'Let judgement run down as waters and righteousness as a mighty stream'.

I began by saying: 'This is a dangerous occasion; civic religion is dangerous.' And went on to expound the prophet's denunciations of injustice and how the poor are denied justice and how the rich bribe lawyers. At the end of the service as I waited at the main door to greet the congregation on their way out, the stony-faced judges walked past me and not one shook my hand. Complaints followed. John Andrew asked me for a copy of my sermon to show the archbishop. I had been ordained just one year ago; perhaps I was going to be sacked.

Then I received a handwritten card from the archbishop saying: 'I wish I had preached that.'

For Christmas 1964 I wrote the nativity play, calling it *Full Circle*. It began in a traditional manner with mother and child, crib, angels and shepherds. Then as the Wise Men entered there came a loud rattling at the church door. Several teddy boys appeared and proceeded to disrupt the play. The actors fled, throwing the baby doll Jesus to the ground. The teddy boys wrecked the scenery, complaining coarsely about the play's stupidity and irrelevance. Many in the audience were horrified, not knowing if this was a real disruption or part of the performance. The teddy boys were actors, but still no one could be sure when a member of the congregation stood up and accused the teddy boys of blasphemy then threatened to call the police. A fight broke out and I intervened, bringing the play to an end. The person interrupting the youngsters was also an actor. I then turned to the stunned audience and asked: 'How would you finish the play?' I wanted them to reflect on what it meant to them. They were, however, so upset that no one could address this question and the event concluded in confusion.

As so often in the future I underestimated the effect of my words and events I arranged. Continually accused of being naïve I slowly learned not to mind and continued what I had to do.

In July 1965 Andrew Henderson, a friend from my time at Cuddesdon, suggested I become chaplain to Mervyn Stockwood, Bishop of Southwark. Andrew, son of the Bishop of Bath and Wells, who knew Mervyn Stockwood personally, proposed my name. I met the bishop. He offered me the job and I accepted his invitation.

Southwark

My enthusiasm for this appointment indicated an ambitious streak in my nature. Bored with being a religious 'redcoat', I wanted to 'get on'; being chaplain to a bishop who happened to be a well-known public figure seemed a useful way forward.

I also resented laying clues for treasure hunts around the Wiltshire countryside while my Cambridge friends were flying high. Nicholas Barrington had left for Pakistan as a young diplomat at the High Commission eventually returning to being High Commissioner. Julian Pettifer was already a star reporter for the BBC, ducking bullets in Vietnam.

My ambition perplexed me. What did it mean to become a bishop? I tried on one of Mervyn Stockwood's mitres once, looked in the mirror and felt wrong. It did not fit my face. The archbishop had spoken to me and other deacons before ordaining us, saying: 'Ambition is fine, but don't leave it snarling and unconsecrated.'

Mervyn Stockwood presided over a diocese made famous and controversial by what became known as 'South Bank religion'. Mervyn had no grand plan or strategy. He created a stage on which the new thinking in the Church of England could flourish, a roll-call of celebrated names: John Robinson, Bishop of Woolwich and author of *Honest to God*; David Sheppard, a star cricketer who became ordained and succeeded John Robinson in Woolwich before eventually becoming Bishop of Liverpool; and Hugh Montefiore, Bishop of Kingston, recognized as being in the vanguard of liberal Church thinking from his time as Vicar of Great St Mary's in Cambridge. He subsequently became Bishop of Birmingham. The diocese flourished with a host of clergy many of whose names are now forgotten, but who inspired and influenced a generation of churchgoers. They reflected Mervyn's open-mindedness: John Pearce-Higgins's interest in the paranormal, and radical activists like Eric James, Paul Oestreicher, Nick Stacey at St Mary's Woolwich, Douglas Rhymes whose book *The New Morality* anticipated debates about sexuality, and Stanley Evans, a former communist who was Principal of the Southwark Ordination Course. Though Mervyn made no deliberate effort to create a team, these intellectually formidable minds formed a movement which could be called a New Reformation (the title of one of John Robinson's books). In Southwark especially, though to a lesser extent throughout England, questions were being raised about the organization of the Church of England, new thinking in theology and attempts to create new forms of worship, bringing the ancient liturgy into the modern world. The pioneers in the Southwark Ordination Course (based on the worker priest movement in France) laid the foundation for new training schemes where students remaining in their jobs while continuing studying for ordination.

The excitement generated under the umbrella of the Bishop of Southwark attracted me to the post of chaplain. I got to meet and know many of the 'stars' in Southwark who were later to become friends and colleagues, though at the time, as chaplain, I could only be gate-keeper to the bishop, a go-between.

In Maidstone I had lived in a three-bedroom semi-detached house owned by Ethel Wilson, a retired teacher. She and her nephew, a teacher at Maidstone Grammar School, provided a 'home' for me while I found my clerical legs. As chaplain to the bishop I now lived in a substantial property erected in 1906 in Streatham, the last building on the north side at the corner where Tooting Bec Gardens meets Tooting Bec Common: Bishop's House. I moved into one of the guest rooms where I lived for three years, but never unpacked completely. It was not home.

Seven staff were dedicated to the bishop's welfare: two secretaries, a non-resident housekeeper, a chauffeur, sometimes two gardeners and a cleaner who also ensured that the Episcopal robes were kept in good repair and spotless, as well as the chaplain. Mrs Stockwood, the bishop's mother, lived in a flat on the first floor. The attic had been converted into a tiny chapel where the bishop and chaplain said morning and evening prayers and most days one of us celebrated the Eucharist.

In *Mervyn Stockwood: A Lonely Life*, written a year after the bishop died, his biographer Michael de la Noy describes a complex, contradictory and formidably talented man with a wealth of fact and incident which I need not repeat here. He quotes a pen portrait by Arthur Valle, a Methodist minister who had worked with Mervyn when he was Vicar of St Mathew's Moorfield in Bristol:

> For all his apparently extrovert nature he was an essentially lonely man. For all his seeming arrogance he was humble and even self distrustful deep down. For all his man of the world appearance, inside he was deeply spiritual. For all his enjoyment of the good things of life, he was in fact very self disciplined. For all his seeming assurance he was not without his doubts and uncertainties. And there is no doubt that right inside him was a kind and compassionate heart.[8]

Those who worked closely with Mervyn, like his chaplains, secretaries, fellow bishops and archdeacons, had to negotiate these contradictions and much of de la Noy's biography describes the ways we managed or failed to manage.

Since 1980, when Mervyn retired, there have been three Bishops of Southwark, so younger generations have forgotten what a significant person he had been. The present diocese of South London is almost unrecognizable from what it had been twenty years earlier. A detailed study should be made of the phenomenon of South Bank religion, addressing the important question: To what extent is change affected by individuals or through institutions? Or put it another way: What was the lasting effect of Mervyn Stockwood's ministry, and those whom he gathered around him, on the Church of England?

In April 1967 Mervyn's mother died. She collapsed in the bath. Mervyn and I got her out of the bath, and she remained unconscious for several days. After she had been taken to hospital I entered the drawing room and saw Mervyn looking out of the window, his back to me. Suddenly his shoulders began to shake. He turned round with tears in his eyes. I know I should have gone over, put my arms around him saying everything would be all right. But I could not bring myself to do it. He was an intimidating father figure.

Then in September of the same year my mother died. She was just sixty.

Over the years I visited Chichester when I could. Once my father retired their relationship had begun to disintegrate. My mother began to behave erratically, gave up cooking and drank too much. She had been ill for some years and eventually was diagnosed with a malignant brain tumour. She made a brief recovery after an operation and intensive course of chemotherapy. Mervyn generously gave me all the time I needed to be with her.

During the days of her dying I stayed at home. The local doctor kept to strict rules about dispensing morphine, saying there were limits. Too much and he would be killing her. So, when the end came my mother suffered terrible pain, breathing with difficulty. As she died with a prolonged death rattle my father held one of her hands and I the other, so for a few minutes our little fragile family was united. Wearing my clerical collar I recited the prayers for the dying, the Our Father and the Nunc Dimittis.

When it was all over my father looked at me with moist eyes and said: 'Now I think we should get to know each other.'

Suddenly rage seized hold of me. 'Now?' I exclaimed to myself. 'Now he says this?'

As soon as they had taken the body away I made some excuse and left the house.

I drove to report my mother's death to her sisters, first to Aunty Jane in whose house I had spent many a Christmas as a small boy. I turned the corner and saw the familiar long low Sussex flintstone manor house and suddenly had to stop the car. I got out and sat on the verge.

The house stood at the end of a lane. No traffic passed. A fine warm day, every window in the house was open. The front door was open. I noticed the sheep in the orchard, especially Mary the pet ewe. As a new-born lamb she had been raised by the family, fed from a bottle. The family could not part with her so she stayed close to the house, growing fatter than the other sheep. I noticed the peacocks in the garden, a swan and ducks on the pond in the front garden. Three spaniels belonging to my uncle lay asleep on the porch. They lifted their heads and gazed at me.

I had to stop the car because at that moment I felt completely at one with everything I saw. It was as if my whole world fitted together. The scene evoked a sense of totality, wonder and awe. Then as this fleeting moment passed I experienced an overwhelming sadness. This was not just the death of my mother, but also of the experience which had so briefly touched me: loss, sadness and reassurance.

After the funeral I returned to work and although I visited my father regularly I never stayed at home again.

In a generous gesture of helping me recover after my mother's death, Mervyn took me on an official visit to Christ Church Grosse Point, a wealthy suburb of Detroit in the USA where he had been invited to give several lectures, even though it was not necessary for a chaplain to accompany him.

We stayed with a rich family who could not have been more hospitable, telling us to make ourselves at home. But I forgot to ask for the lavatory. During the night I got up to relieve myself and looked up and down a long corridor with many doors. A flower pot in the room did not seem big enough, so I opened the window and relieved myself on to the drive below. I travelled many times to the States and all over the world in years to come and learned an important lesson for the future: find out before it's too late where the facilities are!

Christ Church Grosse Point had given a large donation to East Side Voice of Independent Detroit (ESVID), established after the Detroit riots. Black militancy, crime, poverty and unemployment sparked off the burning of much of the inner city. The funds were intended for a squad of vigilantes, young men from the streets who had turned themselves into a local police force because the white police were not welcome in their neighbourhood. The congregation of Christ Church Grosse Point feared the money was being spent on arms. They delegated me, a foreigner, to find out what happened to the donation.

I had a long meeting with Frank Ditto, the founder of ESVID, and received no direct answer. Instead he questioned me sharply about inner-city problems in Britain. Feeling defensive about my ignorance I told him what I knew and asked, weakly: 'What do you think we should do?'

'Clean out your own stable!' he said.

I never forgot this reply.

Returning to England with the bishop, our relationship improved. Maybe it was the shared experience of our mothers' deaths that improved our relationship, or perhaps we had just got used to being together. Among many things I learned from him was a capacity for making the best of difficult situations.

Mervyn suffered from a weak chest with chronic asthma and bronchitis. Once, recovering from bronchitis, he decided to hold the weekly staff meeting for the suffragan bishops and archdeacons in his bedroom. Propped up in bed with its purple sheets, purple pillow cases, purple cover and purple pyjamas, he watched me bringing in chairs and placing them around the bed. At coffee time he became restless because of a secret surprise he and I had prepared. I served the bishops and archdeacons coffee. 'Now,' he announced, 'I must take my medicine. My chaplain will bring it.' I brought in a silver tray with a tumbler of something sparkling. He gave me a large wink and drank it all. The others were not supposed to realize it was champagne. But they knew Mervyn well enough.

On another occasion, returning from Dublin where Mervyn had been preaching at St Patrick's Cathedral, the flight experienced such severe turbulence that we all expected to die. Mervyn stood up, gathered himself together and declared: 'If we are going to crash let's have champagne!' And ordered bottles for all the passengers.

Mervyn's ministry inspired me because he pushed the boundaries. As a priest in his parishes in Bristol and Cambridge, then as bishop, he took full advantage of the freedom which came with the job. He exploited the opportunities given him, in ecumenism, in politics, in journalism, and in giving hospitality and support to his clergy. Today this kind of ministry is inconceivable. Bishops now have to manage decline in the Church of England in a predominantly secular world. This means consultations, committees, all invariably serving the lowest common denominator, not least in the way appointments are made. Mervyn possessed a shrewd judgement of people. He did consult, but discreetly, because he had generally already made up his own mind.

In 1968 when it came to the end of my chaplaincy Mervyn suggested first St Matthew's Brixton. However, St Matthew's was in the throes of a building programme and it did not seem right for me. I wanted to work with a team. 'I think St Peter's St Helier would be good,' Mervyn announced. 'I'll have a word with the church wardens.'

I met them briefly and my induction was set for January 1969.

To prepare me for my task as vicar in one of London's largest housing estates, Mervyn suggested I attend the Urban Training Center in Chicago for a five-weeks' course.

Those weeks in Chicago changed me totally and irrevocably.

The doors opened.

Chicago[9]

Throughout the 1968 freedom and liberation uprisings, people in Paris, Prague and Chicago were prepared to stand and be counted.

'Be Realistic: Demand the Impossible' became a common slogan. Across the world from Rome to Mexico City the possibilities of mass action for change were evident. For a few days in Paris an alliance of students, intellectuals, artists and manual workers defied President de Gaulle. A poster appeared on the Paris streets with De Gaulle's face alongside the words: 'Be Young and Shut Up'.

I did not participate in this agitation, but observed its progress on television. 'The whole world is watching,' chanted the protestors as the Battle of Chicago raged over five days while the Democratic Convention took place at the Hilton Hotel in August 1968. The protest halted the convention. Cameras showed police and national guard officers beating up anyone in their way: the elderly, women and children as well as reporters and demonstrators. Cameras followed people with blood pouring from head wounds streaming into the Hilton.

The Yippies, the Youth International Party, arrived in Chicago that August. They planned to launch a Festival of Life in contrast to the Democratic Convention, which they called a Festival of Death. Rumours spread that politicians were going to be kidnapped and that the water supply would be contaminated with LSD. Mayor Dayley of Chicago issued an order to 'shoot to kill'.

Unplanned, the Battle of Chicago became the final demonstration, the final 'happening' of an extraordinary year marking a change of consciousness across the world. While the radicals exploited television as the new global media, they were not able to unite let alone propose strategies for freedom and liberation. As one commentator put it: 'More Groucho Marx than Karl Marx.'

In Chicago and elsewhere protests on a range of issues took place, foremost the anti-Vietnam campaign. By January 1968 sixteen thousand young Americans had been killed in that war. Today reports from Afghanistan and Iraq are packaged and controlled. Then there was no censorship. Americans were not used to seeing their soldiers day after day running scared, suffering and inflicting horrific casualties. A young generation of mostly wealthy and university educated people now broke away from authority and tradition.

The protests and demonstrations lacked coherence. But in the USA they could accurately be described as the collapse of the American Dream, triggered by the Civil Rights Movement in the South, led by Martin Luther King.

Calls to end segregation were expressed, erupting in riots across Watts, Los Angeles, Newark and Detroit along with demands for better schools, health care and job opportunities. Handouts were no longer acceptable. The lifeless ghettoes had been drained of hope.

Meanwhile cities were experiencing strife and confrontation as frequent regular events and on a scale unheard of in Britain.

I arrived in Chicago three months after the Democratic Convention and enrolled as a student at the Urban Training Center (UTC).

UTC had established its headquarters in a ramshackle disused church on Ashland Avenue at the edge of the city ghetto.

There were no frills, no name tags or introductions.

Though well heated for the approaching Chicago winter the rooms were shabby with basic furniture. UTC housed two radical organizations. One a white organization committed to wiping out racism in white institutions, the Committee for One Society; the other a group of about forty black organizations committed to justice and quality, the Black Consortium.

An Episcopal theologian, Gibson Winter, along with two far-seeing Episcopalian bishops, Kilmer Myers of Northern California and Paul Moore of New York, founded the Urban Training Center in 1964. As the crises in the cities escalated they realized there were serious issues confronting urban churches: survival on the one hand, and, on the other, discerning opportunities for clergy and congregations in rapidly changing neighbourhoods now joining the movements for social justice.

American urban churches were no longer the traditionally tranquil islands of stability as held in common memory. The days had gone when a local priest, father figure of a neighbourhood, could wangle a playground or some other amenity through contacts in City Hall. Barry Fitzgerald, Bing Crosby and Gene Kelly used to play these black-suited priests in Hollywood films from the 1950s. Now in the 1960s they belonged to another age.

Within four years UTC had established itself as the leading training agency in the USA, supported by nineteen Protestant denominations, the Roman Catholic Church, the Orthodox Church, many foundations, the University of Chicago and seminaries across the country. Two hundred and fifty students participated annually, either on a short introductory course, like the one I had been sent on, or on a one- to two-year course with placements in community organizations in Chicago.

The students came from all denominations. There were pastors from store-front churches, Pentecostalists and evangelicals of every sort as well as clergy from the mainline denominations and a smattering of clergy who had dropped out of their church to join community organizations.

I was the only foreigner on my course.

There were no women involved then, but that would change later. We arrived with a variety of agendas. Some were asking: 'How can the inner-city church be saved?' 'How can ministers be toughened up?' 'How should congregations respond to the clamour for justice?' And there were broader questions: 'What role could religion play in this revolutionary climate?' 'What new roles might there be for the clergy?'

Students at UTC were highly motivated. No one sent them. The training had a pronounced 'left' bias. Those who voted for Nixon regarded organizations like UTC as dangerous and irresponsible. Mayor Daley had the place bugged, so the rumour ran.

Despite careful planning the programme was liable to disruption by students boycotting seminars they considered dull, stupid and patronizing, or taking them over. Disruption also occurred at unexpected arrivals by Jesse Jackson, then a minister from the West Side of Chicago, or Saul Alinsky, the doyen of citizens' organizations, or the maverick Monsignor Ivan Illich from Cuernavaca. UTC was invariably described as a 'happening', a favourite 1960s word.

I had never experienced such intensity, seriousness and questioning. Heady stuff. All the time we knew we were making history, creating a new tomorrow – as we thought.

The programme began with 'the plunge'.

Immediately on arrival each participant was given two dollars and sent alone into the city for four days.

We were invited to experience Chicago not as a survival course but as a retreat: listening, observing and then reflecting on what we lived through. I walked many miles to find Alice's Restaurant, a legendary centre for the hippy community, but could not find it. One night I slept in a doorway, another in an all-night cinema where the security guard prodded me and other punters every half hour to keep us awake. Then I decamped to the warmth of the Greyhound bus station.

I spent two nights in a flophouse having secured a job in a paint factory which paid for a room. I had no conversations worth recording. Street people do not like being interrogated, and anyhow they found my English accent incomprehensible.

The plunge was crucial in changing my attitudes, opinions and beliefs. I listened to whatever happened to come my way. On the streets I had no need to argue, organize, arrange or plan anything, let alone look after a bishop. So by the time I returned to the programme at UTC I felt free, ready and available to respond to all I heard there. The place buzzed with talk, confrontation and argument. My conservative views and attitudes were now rapidly being eroded and undermined.

Dick Luecke, Director of Studies, devised the programme. He had been Lutheran Chaplain of Princeton University, an inspirational teacher, sharp, tough and highly intelligent, as well as philosopher, theologian and activist.

He describes how he invited his congregation to look at what was happening in nearby American cities such as Philadelphia, Trenton, Paterson and Newark:

All this preacher knew what to do was to say a bit more shrilly each week: 'Look! People who live with the image of the crucified God ought to be able to look at what is happening for ten more minutes.' Until one day a listener stopped at the door to make the obvious comment: 'OK, preacher, you sold me! Now what do we DO?'[10]

Dick left Princeton University for Chicago to put together the Urban Training Center. There he planned to help clergy join people in their attempts to face up to what the forces of the city had done to them and develop projects which could resist or redirect those powers. As he cryptically added in his inimical way: 'Given vehicles for the exercise of freedom and community in the city, it might make sense to preach again!'

The programme had four interrelated parts, which together provided a pattern for working and handling change.

First, students undertook an analysis of the neighbourhood where he or she worked. This involved asking questions such as: 'What is going on here? What is worrying people? Why are people behaving like this? What are the constraints of institutions, locally and nationally? How do voluntary agencies, including the Churches, see their function, and what do they do in practice?'

This analysis had to be completed before arriving at UTC. Though still working for Mervyn Stockwood I had managed to begin an enquiry into life on the St Helier Estate in South London, where I would be working.

This particular process of analysis was designed to highlight emerging issues. Much energy was then given in the second element of the course explaining the difference between 'problems' and 'issues'. Given sufficient resources, technical know-how, agreement and will power, problems can be solved. Thus it could be possible, for example, to build a bridge over the Atlantic. However, problems become an issue at the point of definition when different, even irreconcilable views are expressed, particularly by those who are powerless to change their situation: workers, patients, students, tenants, the poor. I will give an example of this later where I describe more fully the difference between problem and issue at the local general hospital where I worked as unpaid chaplain.

The third element concerned development of a proposal for ministry: action. What plans need to be put together to address the issues? Where are the allies? What resources are available, including those for the church? What other models exist? What are their strengths and weaknesses? How possible or effective will the project be, and does it relate to the issue in question? Where and who are our enemies and what are the specific restraints? How will it be possible for the person initiating and seeing the project through to make time to remain reflective and faithful to the analysis?

The final element in this process was reflection. Dick Luecke urged the participants to stay true to each their own religious tradition, retrieving the basic impulses and convictions, taking fresh resolve and encouragement from them. He often quoted the medieval theologian John of Salisbury, who said: 'We read these ancient texts to improve our eyesight in the present.' We engaged in the practice of 'hermeneutics' (Hermes being the bearer of messages from the gods) and in recovering ancient meanings, judgements and values we placed them alongside the realities of our everyday working lives.

Easier said than done, forty years on I still use this practice.

Semantics became an issue.

It is commonplace to accept that when two nouns are placed together the sense is self-evident. This is not the case. Too much juxtaposition makes reading and listening mind numbing. Take this example: strategy development, a popular phrase. It could mean either 'strategy for development' or 'in development' or 'with development' – all meaning something different. A sentence then carries several meanings at once. So when the aim of UTC is declared: 'to foster faithful participation in cities', this means being down to earth with plans and projects, but also being faithful to tradition, in the manner I described in my comments on reflection. This density and ambiguity does not make for clarity.

The processes of analysis and planning are now called 'scoping' or 'mapping' exercises. But there is a significant difference between the approaches then and now. Analysis then had a subversive quality. Contained within the process itself were questions and concerns that opened possibilities for people to take control even within institutional constraints.

Richard Hauser, an Austrian sociologist who visited Chicago frequently and whom I got to know well later, told us to 'hold on to our curiosity'. He urged us to stick with the questions, find out what is actually happening on the street, in the neighbourhood and city; also to keep note of our indignation, what upsets us in a given situation.

Assumptions about human nature are less hopeful these days. Driven by the need for concrete outcomes, human nature is so often understood in reductionist and mechanistic terms which display a pervasive cynicism.

As I entered the doors of that ramshackle church in Chicago in 1968 I had to decide how to be a lively part of this bedlam. Would I remain a foreigner, an Englishman, observing and offering the occasional intervention from the sidelines?

I decided to let go. I did not hold back and as a representative of a fading British imperialism quickly became the target for several black leaders who demanded to know what 'this fucking limey' was doing in Chicago. I gave as good as I got and joined in the passionate rhetoric and honest scrutiny. In my desire 'to help' I began to be aware of my own racist prejudices, my sense of intrinsic superiority to black people. They made it clear that 'good white liberals' like me were the problem. Night after night we sat together, sharing take-aways, trading insults and then finally often embracing each other.

Those conversations changed me. I found the arguments of the black leaders, some of whom were part of Martin Luther King's inner circle, incontestable. They spoke of continual harassment, brutality by the police, the poverty of the ghettoes. They taught me to look at the world through the eyes of those who are pushed to the edge and outside it. The change in my opinions did not just come from arguments. This happened during those moments of silence in my head when I began to own what I heard.

So much of what took place at the Urban Training Center in the 1960s and early 1970s seemed a vain hope, so little accomplished. Capitalism triumphed. Looked at from the perspective of defeated dreams, all that energy, commotion and excitement seemed an exercise in futility.

However, the hopes and processes shared there were taken across the world by a generation of young idealists, including myself. When I returned to England I determined to establish an Urban Training Center in London.

First I had to start my new job and put into practice what I had learned in Chicago. On 29th January 1969 I was inducted as Vicar of St Peter's on the St Helier Estate in Morden on the southern edge of Greater London.

Vicar

After moving home nine times in ten years it came as a relief to settle in the vicarage behind St Peter's Church in January 1969. The vicarage had been built in 1934, when the St Helier Estate had been completed; it is a slightly larger version of what were then council houses.

The estate was designed as a 'garden city' for people being re-housed from the slums of inner London, so open spaces were planned on a lavish scale. Each of the ten thousand houses had a strip of garden. For just sixpence in the 1960s, workmen could get to Central London by underground.

Nearly thirty thousand people lived on the estate which now became my parish. The place was dominated by the St Helier Hospital, birthplace of the future Prime Minister John Major and a landmark on the South London skyline. During the Second World War this monumental white building had to be painted black in order to confuse the Luftwaffe on their bombing raids to London.

Visiting the council officials in County Hall to find out how they regarded the estate and its tenants I was told: 'St Helier has been one of the best. People never complain. It's a peaceful place. The tenants never cause any trouble.'

Rent books were packed with strictly enforced rules. Tenants were not allowed to 'drive nails or allow or permit nails to be driven into the walls of the premises', neither could they 'lay linoleum on any wooden floor within one foot of any wall during the first year of tenancy. But the border may be stained if desired.' Tenants were required to clean their windows weekly, and the chimney swept annually. They were entitled to 'use the back garden as a drying ground for their own washing, but shall not otherwise expose to public view or hang out from the windows any washing or unsightly objects'. Ominously the tenancy agreement makes it clear that 'duly authorized officers' can have access 'at any time 'to check the 'regulations are being observed'.

In spite of the careful thought in designing the estate there were few places where people could meet, just a launderette and a couple of pubs, one of which, the St Helier Arms, was not for the faint-hearted. There were infrequent buses to Morden underground station. Lack of transport and community amenities created problems.

Nothing could have been more different from my experience of inner-city Chicago. Then remembering Richard Hauser's advice to 'harness my curiosity' I soon discovered there was more to the St Helier than a drab housing estate.

I wanted to get on with the work, so furnished the house quickly and modestly. A retired priest gave me a large walnut dining room table and six chairs.

I paid particular attention to my study, making it comfortable and inviting. Across the corridor from the study stood the parish office, which contained a dilapidated Gestetner printing machine, a few files and an antique Remington typewriter. 'Muriel will come and do typing for you,' I was told.

At the induction service in a packed church John Robinson, then Bishop of Woolwich, preached on a text from the Beatles: *Let It Be*. He became a regular visitor to St Peter's and when appointed Dean of Trinity College, Cambridge he bought a house nearby in Reigate. He officiated at the Christmas Eve Midnight Mass with gravitas and simplicity but was shy and sometimes inept socially. After Midnight Mass, attending a party in the vicarage, I once overheard him talking to one of my church wardens, a plumber, who had never taken a holiday much further than Southend. 'So where are you going skiing this year?' the bishop asked him.

Mervyn Stockwood performed the Institution, a term used to describe the admission of a new incumbent to the 'care of souls in this parish', not to the congregation, but to the geographical parish, in this case the St Helier Estate.

The bishop began the service with the words: 'I ask you to pray with me that Donald may be a faithful priest, a wise and fearless leader and a true shepherd of God's people.'

I felt apprehensive. The church wardens had met me only once and had to go along with the bishop's recommendation that I should be their vicar. There had been no job description, no formal interview. I had been parachuted on to their estate.

There is no ABC about how to be a vicar. What had I let myself in for? Would I be expected to perform the role of a religious red-coat as at Maidstone? At the same time I was determined to translate my Chicago experience to St Helier.

Weddings and funerals dominated the weekly routine. Funerals in particular. No one had warned me there would be around two hundred and fifty funerals a year – not surprising since 30 per cent of the population were over sixty.

Alan Bennett in *Untold Stories* relates his experience of municipal crematoria: the setting was 'soft enough to make something so raw as grief seem out of place. It's harder to weep where there's a fitted carpet.' He describes the service as 'un-solemn, hygienic and somehow retail, the service is so scant as to be scarcely a ceremony at all, and is not so much simple as inadequate'.[11]

What he cannot describe is how it felt to take a funeral service in this environment where as he writes: 'everything is tidied away'.

Often I wanted to stop reading the prayers and say to the congregation, rarely more than a dozen: 'Hey! Let's give George a really good send-off. Don't let this awful place inhibit you. Weep, cry, shout! Do whatever you want . . . do something!'

Instead I tried to make an occasion they would remember, taking them carefully through the service, the Burial of the Dead in the Book of Common Prayer. I always asked if anyone wanted to say anything. Rarely did anyone respond. Crematoria do not encourage spontaneity. And people are shy, not used to being close up to a vicar. They would try to sing 'Abide With Me'; also 'Dear Lord and Father of Mankind'. The latter has nothing to do with death or eternal life, but Parry's tune is reassuring, easier to whistle than to sing.

Beginning a practice I have continued every since, I told those small congregations in the North East Surrey Crematorium about the authors of the hymns, the composers of the music and how the words and music met. These stories improve the quality of the singing. Years later at a memorial service at St James's Piccadilly, as I shook hands with the congregation coming out of the church, an elderly businessman congratulated me: 'Well, Padre, you will always be remembered for what you said about the hymns!'

When, as so often happened at the North East Surrey Crematorium, I had to conduct two or three funerals in a row I would try to talk to the crematorium staff, but the conversation was desultory. Rather than talk to an earnest young vicar they preferred to leaf through stacks of pornography while waiting for the next coffin to arrive.

Once I forgot a funeral. The Bishop of Southwark received complaints. He called to reassure me that he had done the same. Mervyn used to phone me regularly during my first months at St Peter's, to encourage and support me. Knowing my taste in food he would always ask: 'And have you got enough marmalade?' This time he promised to write to the family and told me to visit the widow and apologize. When I arrived, nervous and guilty, she did not seem bothered. 'Come in and have a nice cup of tea!' she said.

Anxious to make amends I offered to bring her the reserved sacrament once a month. For five years we established an unusual ritual. 'We'll have a nice cup of tea,' she would say when I arrived. 'Thank you,' I'd reply, 'we can have it after the service.' 'I'll go and put the kettle on,' she'd say. I recited some prayers. But she would be listening out for the whistle, which indicated the water was boiling, so she never paid much attention to the prayers. When I gave her the consecrated wafer with the words 'The body of Christ', she took it, opened a large black handbag, dropped it in, snapped the bag shut and said: 'I think tea's ready.' After some months I realized she had no idea what I was doing. She eventually told me she had never been to church. But having started I did not know how to extricate myself from this performance. My visits were all that mattered to her. I never discovered what she did with the wafers.

When visiting the bereaved after a funeral and arriving unannounced they gave me a guarded welcome. Clergy are reminders of death, provoking memories they wanted to forget. We were just part of the 'service', along with the undertakers.

Funerals and parish work were shared among three clergy. One was priest-in-charge of Bishop Andrewes, another church on the estate, also part of the parish; the other two were curates attached to St Peter's.

Shortly after my arrival John Robinson introduced me to Dr Una Kroll.

Una had been called to the priesthood since the age of nineteen. She trained as a doctor and because she could not be ordained, became a nun, joining a missionary order that sent her to be a nun-doctor in Liberia. Eventually she left the order, married and had four children. She then worked as a family doctor in England.

The first woman to be trained at the Southwark Ordination Course, Una knew she could not be ordained. She had nowhere to go as a deaconess after completing the course. Una describes how she arrived at St Peter's Church in a letter to Eric James, published in his biography of John Robinson (*A Life of Bishop John AT Robinson*):

> John matched me with a parish priest in Morden called Donald Reeves. He was a creative genius as well as being young and eccentric enough to accept a wounded feminist on his staff. Probably no one else could have offered me such a generous home where I could learn and make mistakes as Donald did for the first ten years of my active ministry.

As soon as Una with Leo, her husband came into my study I knew that they would both be welcome, and saw at once that women should be ordained. Up to that moment I had not thought much about the ordination of women. I read subsequently all the arguments for and against, but that initial meeting was decisive.

Playing a small part in the Movement for the Ordination of Women I sat with Una in November 1978 at the General Synod in Church House when she called down from the gallery: 'We asked for bread; you gave us a stone!' As a member of the General Synod in November 1992 I took part in the historic vote that allowed the ordination of women. As I left Church House in a blaze of TV lights I overheard one woman say to another: 'He's all right, he's one of us.'

Not all the clergy nor congregation at St Peter's accepted the idea of a woman as priest or bishop, and the issue often made for difficult times. I quickly learned that women were not the problem, but the men. That is another story.

In October 1974 at the second General Election that year, Una stood as a candidate for the Women's Rights Campaign in the constituency for Sutton and Cheam. Invited to join her all-woman campaign team I was initiated into a new way of running meetings. These could be long and intense, everyone joining in and being listened to with equal attention. The power of the question was respected. Being the only man in the room they tolerated me and I began to realize how it must feel to be a token woman on committees. I had no one to look at, no other man whose eye I could catch. Meetings lacked any agenda I could recognize but after four or five hours crammed in the Krolls' front room everything had been covered and agreed.

The campaign assigned me the job of 'door knocking' in the more affluent diehard Tory parts of Cheam. Striding around in my cassock with a suffragette sash I enjoyed my doorstep confrontations with traditional views: 'a woman's role is in the home and women's rights have no place there' (Una and other women had been working to change the Sex Discrimination and Equal Opportunities Act). Una got just two hundred and ninety-eight votes. The Conservatives were returned with a massive majority.

I lunched with Una regularly. She allowed herself just one hour and in that time she helped Leo prepare the food, took messages from her practice as a GP in Merton, returned calls to journalists, attended to her children and in the midst of all these activities carried on significant conversations with me. I have never met anyone who could do so many things at once. And she was a prolific writer.

When she came to preach at St James's Church, Piccadilly, before her ordination as a priest in the Church of Wales, I welcomed her as 'my bishop' – much to her astonishment.

Una and Leo became part of a team at St Peter's. For a number of years there would be seven or eight clergy at any one time, honorary, part time as well as three or four on the staff. In twelve years nineteen clergy passed through the parish. Two became bishops, one a headmaster and one a dean.

Apart from attending a short course on Management by Objectives organized by the Industrial Society I had no experience of leading or managing. I set myself targets and encouraged the team to do the same, as a way of creating some shape to a life of many roles and activities, but the language of business did not suit parish work. We were not managers inflicting targets on unsuspecting parishioners. After six years I abandoned this method and tried to work in a more organic way.

Much time and emotional energy was spent trying to create a lively and agreeable working group. Disagreements meant we had on occasion to call on the services of a consultant therapist. Since this was the age of psychobabble he would remark: 'What I think I hear you saying' and then proceed to reveal what he interpreted to be, say, an attack on me, 'the father', and Una, 'the mother'. Silence greeted these comments either because, as I discovered later, they were considered to be nonsense, or so profound as to need digesting. I found psychobabble interesting but neither life-changing nor illuminating.

Meanwhile there was a wide gap between the activities of the clerical team, and the congregation and the parish. Most of the congregational activities were social: weekly bingo, a drama group, a social club, a lunch club for the elderly, the choir, Sunday school, girl guides, brownies and scouts all organized and run by people living on the St Helier Estate. They flourished without the benefit of a single cleric, let alone seven of us.

We often spoke about 'enabling' and working with people, but in spite of our best intentions we tended to plan activities at people. The congregation was practised at ignoring the latest vicar's bright ideas. Sometimes after I preached a strong sermon on some contemporary issue seventy-five-year-old Mrs Polybank, sitting in her wheelchair by the front row, would comment loudly: 'Donald, you are looking very tired today!'

Reasons for resistance to innovation were plain. We were a colonial outpost, financed and sent by something called the Church of England. Clergy came and went. We had a choice. Most of the tenants on the estate had no choice. They were expected to put up and shut up: 'count your blessings'. They did not see the church as being on their side: 'It doesn't really bother about us.' There when needed, it was otherwise 'just for those who like that sort of thing'.

On my second day at St Peter's, in the middle of unpacking my books, I heard a knock on the door. An elderly lady asked to speak with me. Her husband had just died. Her family had lived opposite the church since 1933. They were not church goers. 'Could I bring him into your church?' she asked. *Your* church, not *our* church. I had been there two days; she had lived there thirty-six years.

I set about completing the situation analysis I began before going to Chicago.

At once I identified the main problem. This was the powerlessness of people as tenants, patients or parents to change or take some control of their lives. Apart from a weak tenants' association there were no organizations with any clout which were able to address specific problems. Words like 'oppression' are over-inflated, but I met in many conversations much apathy, which sometimes is described as 'frozen violence', frustration and anger, a kind of 'exploding apathy'. When a Conservative councillor announced that 'the St Helier Estate had come to the end of its useful life' there was outrage, but in this large, white working-class housing estate there were no organizations where this anger could be channelled and a strategy agreed for a proper process of consultation.

My Christian convictions continued to blossom out of the prophetic tradition which exposed the lies of capitalism and beckoned towards a promise, towards a higher vision of ourselves and of our society. Our task was to offer and if necessary confront the situation with something better, to help people realize that we all have a clear if seemingly impossible objective; and be ready to go to the end of the world with however little backing.

My colleagues and I began to show up in unusual and untypical situations. We organized and helped to organize all kinds of petitions and protests, attended public meetings, and established a community newspaper. I met local, usually apprentice, journalists, regularly, both to find out what was happening and to ensure that they publicized our work. The media marked me then as a swinging, controversial and red vicar, a reputation that lasted well beyond my days on the St Helier Estate.

In my first year I had two opportunities to make our concerns known to a wider audience. First came a television broadcast service, then a People's Service on Radio 2.

Taking care not to criticize the people of the estate, I nonetheless managed to offend some of the people with whom I aimed to be in solidarity. In my televised sermon I described the suicide of an elderly woman who lived near the church. Her note said: 'I feel so alone. I can't go on.' People considered my sermon to be patronizing and I was summoned to a meeting of the now burgeoning tenants' association to explain myself. They criticized me for being a self-appointed community leader who had been on the St Helier Estate for less than half a year. They were right. I should have given more time to build a wider and stronger base from which to speak on behalf of the people. I may have been fearless, but I lacked wisdom and experience. Because they recognized my intentions to be honourable we resolved the matter amicably. I continued to support the association and went on a steep learning curve while working with my fellow clergy to dispel apathy and mobilize latent anger and resentment.

A year later I drove a friend round the estate. Suddenly I stopped and much to her surprise announced: 'This is the most important place in the world for me.'

As I began to speak about the Chicago principles both in St Helier and elsewhere I noticed that my audiences were mystified by my description of the difference between a 'problem' and an 'issue' (see page 70).

But the difference became clear when I described my job as the unpaid chaplain to St Helier Hospital. My duty was to visit patients.

I had been learning new ways of thinking about health other than being just an absence of illness. I understood health as 'wholeness'. This became the issue: I observed the hospital being run as a factory, maximizing 'patient through-put'. This was well before the days when market forces took over. An assistant matron on returning from a course on hospital management told me quite seriously that she felt the hospital would run more smoothly without patients, then realized the foolishness of what she had said.

A more organic approach to healing was needed. Patients should participate in their recovery. I organized seminars on 'keeping healthy', and at the nursing school arranged seminars for doctors and nurses on coping with dying and death. We planned a celebration of health to take place in the hospital.

The hospital porters were then threatening strike action and considered me an ally because I had criticized the hierarchical organization of the hospital, with the patient at the base of the pyramid.

Una commented on my concerns in a letter she wrote to me as I was writing this section:

I was privileged during my ten years as one of the team at St Peter's Morden, in that I was both an independent medical practitioner with considerable responsibility and a member of team in which I was considerably disadvantaged: since I was a woman and a lay person, albeit a deaconess, a person who had no mandate for my own practice.

Before I met you I had assumed that my extensive training and many years experience of general practice gave me the right to give strong advice to patients. Consequently, if patients did not take my advice I felt they were wrong to do so. I would continue to care for them, repeat my advice and remain ready to assist in any way I could, but internally I felt angry both on their behalf and on my own for the consequences of their rejection of my advice could be costly to both parties.

Your ferocious alignment with the patient's point of view gave me new insights in to the way in which respect for the patient's views could lead to a more fruitful partnership. So I came to a position where I did not dismiss the patient's attitude, but began to look at the underlying causes of those attitudes. I learnt to see their complaints about allopathic medicine, the kind practiced by most family doctors, against a background of fear, conflict of interest within the context of their lives, as of great importance. I learnt to approach all my patients within the context of their families, environmental situations and working practices and to treat all patients as partners in the search for health and well-being.

At the hospital my ideas were attracting interest. The hospital management was not pleased and sacked me. 'Padre,' the governor of the hospital told me, 'I can see you are not happy here . . .'

But throughout the hospital, people had begun to think differently about health and the relationship between patients and nurses and doctors.

At my first meeting with the church wardens they expressed concern with the state of the church building.

Designed by Charles Nicholson and built in 1933 the architect wrote for the consecration service:

'"Let me see," said Mr Pecksniff, "you will find some bricks in the back garden; now suppose you put them together with something that will remind us, say, of St Peter's Rome."

Such is the task of the present day builders of churches in growing districts. Any efforts at originality or elaboration have been eschewed. The church had to be fairly large and available funds were not inexhaustible. Therefore since very high buildings are costly and wide buildings look very squat, St Peter's has been built long. It would have been fifteen feet longer had it not been for the restraining influence of an advisory committee.'

From outside, in spite of the architect's ambition, the church looked like a long low barn. Inside the walls were a dingy dirty cream. The building had received no maintenance since 1933. Because it would have been too expensive to heat the church in the winter months the congregation of eighty or so crammed in the church hall and the church had to be locked for fear of vandals.

Initially I considered proposing the sale of the sites of St Peter's, the Catholic and Methodist churches and building a Christian centre for all denominations. This made sense economically. But traditional faith loyalties die hard and I realized that such a radical solution would monopolize all my efforts. There was no way in which St Peter's could be efficiently converted into a multi-purpose building.

Making the best of what existed, redecorating the interior and filling it with pictures so at the least the inside would be like a jewel in a drab landscape: that was the best solution.

Remembering my conversations with Walter Hussey, Dean of

Chichester, I was determined to find a talented, unknown artist who dreamed of painting a church.

So in 1972 Peter Pelz was commissioned to paint the *Stations of the Cross* for St Peter's Church. The pictures were unveiled in June 1973 by Jennie Lee, the former Minister for the Arts, in the presence of a large congregation and the Bishop of Southwark.

The event took place at a time of much media exposure. I had been appearing regularly in television documentaries and discussion programmes. In four years at Morden we had three broadcast services and the cameras had been in on other occasions to film parts of the liturgy. London Weekend Television, completing a fifty-minute documentary about St Peter's on the day of the unveiling ceremony, managed to film the service and the *Stations of the Cross*.

Grand occasions, however well rehearsed, have their difficult moments. The television crew turning up late upset the flower arrangements. The local mayors of Sutton and Merton arrived in their separate cars at the same time from opposite directions, only just managing to avoid a collision. Members of the youth club were dispatched on their motorbikes to act as outriders for the bishop's car; and in their enthusiasm forgot the warning not to exceed twenty miles an hour and shot off at fifty miles an hour, unaware of the bishop's driver trying to keep up behind them.

Jennie Lee congratulated the church on commissioning what she described as 'modern art'. A feature in the *Sunday Telegraph* described the ten *Stations of the Cross*, Crucifixion and Resurrection as 'one of the most arresting displays of modern painting to be found in an English church' (*Sunday Telegraph*, July 1973). Peter Pelz completed his work at St Peter's with a *Nativity* (1975), an *Annunciation* (1976), a painting on the organ case and finally an external mural on the

West front of the *Last Judgement* (1977).

Initial reactions to the paintings were bewildered and hostile. Over the years understanding has grown. 'They mean more to me than most sermons,' I was told. 'They make you think.' 'It's what we all have to go through,' was a frequent observation. Some of the most attentive moments in the Sunday worship have been when the pictures were used in the sermons and opportunities found to lead those coming to the church for the first time into their meaning. The artist provided words to accompany each painting, not to describe but to unlock their meaning. So with the *First Fall Under the Cross*, depicting a modern city being carried Atlas-like on the shoulders of a Christ figure with a new world in the distance waiting to be reborn, Peter Pelz writes:

> The gigantic weight of the city pulls me down – only a super-human effort can lift me through the black of concrete, of obligation and tradition, of competition and survival. There in the distance I glimpse the hope of a new world into which I long to be reborn. It is a world where I can see and feel the sun, where I may grow gently and fully at becoming at one with myself, with others and the universe. But this world pulls me down again. I fall under the terrible burden. And yet my eyes have seen the beauty.

The pictures depict a contemporary world. The St Helier Estate is in every picture, the houses and open spaces along with people from the congregation and neighbourhood. The Cross is not shown anywhere. The artist aimed to get behind the symbolism and portray the raw edges of rejection and suffering. The painful journey from the Last Supper to Crucifixion and Resurrection is made more personal by being shown against the environment of a hostile city familiar to everyone looking. Christ is depicted naked throughout to emphasize his human vulnerability.

The story of the Morden paintings does not have a happy ending.

Seventeen years later a new vicar of St Peter's requested a faculty to remove all the pictures and a consistory court was held to decide their fate.

I did not attend or return to the parish but mustered a substantial array of qualified witnesses and experts to join members of the congregation who were intent on defending their pictures.

John Drury, Dean of King's College, Cambridge, who had just been appointed Dean of Christchurch Oxford, and Leonard Rosoman, a Royal Academy artist, best known for his murals in Lambeth Palace, both spoke, in the words of the presiding chancellor's judgement, 'enthusiastically, and in a manner which showed deep thought about the quality of the pictures and the desirability of retaining them in their present position'.

Judith Collins, Curator of Modern British Art at the Tate Gallery, expressed a visceral dislike of the paintings. The chancellor noted: 'It was clear that Dr Collins did not like the style of Mr Pelz's work and thought its quality unformed and undistinguished.'

The chancellor decreed a faculty for the *Stations of the Cross* to be taken down because the vicar and the Parochial Church Council 'found that the pictures hindered his pastoral work', though adding that he preferred 'the evidence on artistic merit given by Mr Rosoman and Dr Drury', concluding his judgement by observing 'there is no doubt this is a remarkable set of pictures'.

However, the chancellor insisted that the faculty 'will be subject to a condition that provision is made for the storage and preservation of these pictures, pending a faculty for their suitable disposal'.

I have tried to discover what happened to the paintings. They may have been disposed of without another faculty being granted. If so, then inadvertently or deliberately the chancellor's ruling has been ignored. If these paintings have been destroyed then this is an act of vandalism.

This story is a warning to clergy who wish to commission works of art. Peter Burman, then Director of Conservation Studies at the Institute of Advanced Architectural Studies, York University, and Chair of the St Paul's Cathedral Fabric Committee and a member of two others, Durham and Lincoln, in a written submission praising the paintings asked two questions: 'If permission were given for their permanent removal, what would happen to them? And what message would their permanent removal send to artists, and what sort of indication would it give to donors or patrons of fine new works of art in churches?' He adds: 'their permanent removal would cause me great sadness'.

The *Stations of the Cross* could be taken down because they had been painted on wooden panels. However, the request for the removal of the *Last Judgement* mural from the West front of the church meant destruction of the painting. The chancellor describes the mural in a vivid and optimistic way: 'In the Last Judgement Christ is seen as the rising sun, liberating the souls of the faithful at the last day, enabling the faithful to leap heavenwards.' The chancellor dismissed the petition. As he put it: 'It is already a landmark and in this part of London landmarks of such interest and artistic distinction are too rare for the court to sanction the removal of one as striking and significant as this one.'

The mural can still be seen. It has never been vandalized.

In 1976 Julia Usher was commissioned to compose *A Dance for the Son Rising*, 'A Mass for Dancing'. Inspired by the *Stations of the Cross*, specifically the *Resurrection*, *A Dance for the Son Rising* was a setting of the Mass to be danced and sung.[12]

The commission grew organically out of the liturgy celebrated at St Peter's. Over the years much effort had been made to ensure that celebrations on Christmas Eve, Easter Day, Whitsun and the Patronal Festival were prepared by the congregation. Up to forty people were involved in creating them: banners made, special hymns written, readings dramatized, the church decorated. One elderly parishioner told me with a laugh that she brought sunglasses along on Christmas Eve because of the five hundred candles lit around the church. The intention of these communal celebrations was to deepen and intensify traditional elements of worship.

Celebrations at St Peter's always provoked comment. After one Christmas Eve two people wrote to me:

I can't explain it. It was something I shall never forget. It took you out of yourself. Everything – all my life fell into place.

More like a performance than a church service. So much going on. It was like a bloody circus!

When liturgy involves the imagination at this level of communal creativity; when the setting is right, when a church building looks as if a celebration is going to happen, when everything is expressed through stories and images, when the church smells right with incense or other kinds of fragrance; when all these are in place, then it would be odd if there were no dance.

Margaret Stevens, who pioneered a revival of liturgical dance in cathedrals and parishes during the 1960s and 1970s, agreed to create a dance group from the congregation at St Peter's. She disapproved of the charismatic style of repetitive arm movement 'like windmills'. She emphasized the unity of body, mind and spirit, the importance of gesture and movement emanating from the body's centre, movement and dance beginning and ending in stillness.

Having worked with Margaret for some years it seemed a natural development to find a composer for a Mass to be danced – danced and sung.

This commission was unique in musical history and the history of the church. My friend the composer Peter Dickinson, now Professor of Music at Keele University, agreed to help draw up a shortlist and be part of the selection committee. We looked for an unrecognized composer and eventually Julia Usher was offered the commission. She had studied music at Cambridge and York Universities, and been taught by Robert Sherlaw Johnson, a pupil of Messiaen. Living within easy reach of St Peter's she could also bring the Mass to birth as well as compose the music.

Hilary Hunt, a member of the St Peter's Dance Group trained by Margaret Stevens and a teacher with considerable experience of dance and drama, developed the choreography. Though Julia Usher based her music on the traditional structure of the Mass it was felt the Latin words were not enough, yet the words of the new liturgies were inadequate. There would be a distribution of bread and wine, blessed by a priest who performed as one of the dancers, so while describing the event as a Mass might not be strictly accurate it was a sharing or an Agape. David Scott, a priest poet, wrote the words for the Mass.[13]

At the blessing of the bread and wine the celebrant recited:

Blessed be the humble hands that take bread
Blessed be the singing eyes that taste wine
Blessed be the poor hands that feel the body in the bread
Blessed be the pure eyes that see the tears in the wine.
Holy was the bread   Body Divine
Holy were the tears   Shed in the Wine
Holy is the life blood
Soon to be mine.

We gave the composer all the resources she wanted. I told her if she needed a fleet of harps they would be found. The Mass was scored for brass and wind ensemble, percussion, strings, piano, recorders, organ, double choir and a consort of viols.

The Inner London Education Authority's Centre for Young Musicians, a school for the most musically gifted schoolchildren in London, provided forty players.

Despite careful publicity the critics totally ignored the event.

Just as Peter Pelz's *Stations of the Cross* were intended for those unaccustomed to 'looking' at pictures, Julia Usher's music reached out to those unfamiliar with contemporary music. The Mass compelled attention because of its directness and intensity, rooted in Messiaen and music of the East. At one point the dancers were asked to become whirling Dervishes. Some parishioners were disturbed by the elemental Dionysian quality of the Kyrie and Gloria ('music of the Devil', said one of the singers), but the variety of sound and movement conveyed the sense of a community working together. At other moments in a work lasting an hour and a half, the music provided restrained and reflective contrast matched by simple and formal movements. So at the Offertory a long trombone solo, interrupted by horns, echoed the sound of Venetian church bells on a Sunday morning. A member of the congregation commented afterwards: 'It was like watching a village coming to life. By the time the Mass was over I felt I knew everyone.'

Music, words, performers and the church blended totally. They showed in the words of the composer, a Quaker, what she also saw in the *Stations of the Cross*: 'that of God in every man'.

The dancers and singers prepared four months for the Mass. At the performance, writhing on the floor during the Kyrie, releasing ourselves from invisible chains, I was more worried about getting splinters in my feet. And learning to whirl, which is a life-time's vocation for a Dervish, we could only hint at how it could be.

Both the artist and the composer developed a close relationship with the community. Peter Pelz moved into the vicarage and stayed. He ran art classes for people from the St Helier Estate. Young and old, school children and pensioners attended together. Julia Usher became composer-in-residence during preparation for the Mass. Both artists had to work at shaping and sharing their vision with those unused to 'looking' and 'listening'.

There is a possibility of nurture and encouragement for the artist in this relationship, an exchange between the artist and the public where growth of mutual trust enriches both.

Bringing Chicago to England

Meanwhile it had been my intention to establish an Urban Training Center, along the lines of my Chicago experience, in England.

Canon Eric James, an experienced networker in the Church of England and one of the few priests to spend his life doing everything possible to keep the plight of inner cities and their churches in the public eye, introduced me to Tony Dyson, Principal of Ripon Hall Theological College in Oxford.

Inheriting a teaching syllabus with a rural nineteenth-century context, Tony Dyson was determined that the academic training for ordinands take the urban context of the mid-twentieth century seriously and that this context be integrated into the academic programme.

Ripon College linked with St Peter's. Students spent six weeks of their course in London and Morden drawing on the methodology I had learned in Chicago. We established the Urban Ministry Project (UMP) and David Sheppard, then Bishop of Woolwich, became our Chair.

Inevitably the radical edge which had inspired me so much in Chicago was quickly blunted. The protests of the 1960s, arising out of opposition to the Vietnam War, and the Civil Rights Movement in the USA, were more muted in London, with the exception of riots outside the American Embassy on 17th March 1968. 'Sleepy London town' Mick Jagger described the capital accurately in 'Street Fighting Man'.

Though Harold Wilson supported American intervention in Vietnam he refused to commit troops. Protests and Civil Rights issues were on a smaller scale in England. We had no Martin Luther King, no Saul Alinsky. There was little sign of the counter-cultural phenomenon on the St Helier Estate! Moreover, nationally the Labour Party and trade unions saw their struggle in the workplace, on the shop floor, and were sceptical of middle-class idealists and community development.

The Urban Ministry Project's training for ordinands quickly expanded to working clergy and laypeople. Over the next ten years over three hundred and fifty participated in courses that lasted from six to nine months. We experimented with design and content, but the core remained constant: completing a thorough analysis of the neighbourhood where the person worked, gathering a group together from the congregation or colleagues and beyond, leading to the creation of a profile which would bring to light those issues needing attention.

UMP took care to commission independent appraisals and people's work on the analysis was appreciated. Two or three residential sessions followed with input from consultants. The main body of work was done at home or place of work. One priest said: 'I used to feel I was in a cocoon; now I have a handle on how to approach the problems in my parish: homelessness, poverty and no jobs.'

UMP employed consultants for different aspects of the programme. These included economists and sociologists as well as theologians. We visited the clergy in their parishes to encourage and advise on how to create a profile. While in the USA most of the mainline churches had abandoned the ghettos to pitch camp in the more prosperous and settled suburbs, Anglican clergy stayed put. Priests found it difficult to be on the edge of society where churches were marginalized and many felt drained by a sense of failure, regularly leading the same elderly group in worship inside draughty Victorian buildings needing unaffordable restoration. Effort seemed pointless and wasted. Personal problems of the clergy inevitably emerged and we had to address these as a priority.

By the mid-1970s community projects were in retrenchment. Moribund public institutions needed systematic reform. Adventure playgrounds, housing projects, community newspapers, and law centres, to name a few projects emerging from UMP courses, were simply inadequate to deal with larger social issues: rising unemployment; collapse of traditional industries, mining, steel production and shipbuilding; and the effect of all this on communities across the country; a situation later exacerbated by ruthless cuts and closures in the 1980s.

However, UMP sought to empower the clergy in these critical situations, to discover opportunities where only apathy seemed to exist; to draw on the strength of the people that made up their parish, not just a dwindling congregation, but also those outside the churches. As in Chicago, UMP aimed to open our eyes to political, economic and social realities. We also drew on the experience of artists and writers, using drama and the imagination to create deeper understandings of the situation, personally and communally, to nourish and sustain the spirit. For some participants these became significant events which gave meaning to the project and to their ministries.

Inspired by the Civil Rights and liberation movements, UMP was born from a dissenting tradition. This made it unpopular. Newspaper headlines seized on the Plunge, incorporated from the Chicago experience, and ignored the substance of our courses. 'Here Endeth the Doss-in for the Revs' mocked the *Sun*, and more sedately from *The Times*: 'Shock Treatment for the Clergy'. We were regarded as 'too radical' and they accused me of promoting a cheap social gospel with a confused theology.

In retrospect we should have paid more attention to ecumenical issues and created a network that involved laypeople as well as clergy. We were pioneers and made mistakes. I was disappointed that we became stuck in the training mode and failed to become a movement for change. But we drew out the best in many of those who had to work in tough parishes.[14]

In 1979 we celebrated UMP's tenth anniversary.

Donald Coggan, then Archbishop of Canterbury, attended as guest-of-honour. We discussed what work I should do next. I felt I had done what I could at St Peter's and was applying for other jobs, including Head of Religious Broadcasting at the BBC. Apart from my experience of television in front of the cameras I had been Anglican representative on religious programmes for five years on the Independent Broadcasting Authority's Advisory Panel. I understood media politics and the issues around the broadcasting of religious programmes, but a decision had been made not to appoint another Anglican and Colin Morris, a Methodist, was appointed.

The next move in my life happened through the auspices of Kenneth Woollcombe, then Bishop of Oxford. He was a patron of the Urban Ministry Project and lived in Cuddesdon, close to the Theological College, which had just combined with Ripon Hall. Students continued to be involved in UMP courses and the bishop observed me at work.

His first wife had died in 1976. He resigned as Bishop of Oxford, remarried in 1980 and was asked to be Rector of St James's Piccadilly. With a baby on the way he turned the job down. 'I wouldn't know what to do,' he told me. 'And it would not be the best place to bring up a child. This is the job for you.'

St James's had the reputation of being a church famous for stylish weddings. I passed it occasionally when walking down Piccadilly and noted how the place always seemed to be closed.

Kenneth Woollcombe discussed the possibility of my appointment with Gerald Ellison, Bishop of London, who after asking Mervyn Stockwood about my suitability, summoned me for an interview. He had no particular questions but one requirement: 'You must keep the church open; I don't care what you do, but open it must be.'

I had a brief meeting with the church wardens of St James's. One happened to be the Bishop of London's sister and married to a former rector. The other was the bishop's nephew.

At the peak of my energies, aged forty-five, and excited by the challenges and possibilities presented by this Central London church, I gladly accepted the bishop's offer. There was also a bonus. Many livings in the London diocese had been suspended; vicars or rectors were appointed priests-in-charge with contracts that could be renewed or not by the bishop. But I had the freehold of St James's. It would be difficult to get rid of me.

I left St Peter's in July and on 4th November 1980 was inducted as Rector of St James's Piccadilly.

PART TWO

Piccadilly Parson

'St James's Church – now where's that?' said the cab driver, entering Piccadilly from Hyde Park Corner. 'It's the church on the right, set back from the road,' I explained. 'Ah, yes,' he said after a moment's thought, 'it's where the brass rubbing goes on.'

The driver had ferried people round the London streets for over twenty years but the church had not registered: St James's Piccadilly, the best kept secret in London.

On my arrival I could see no justification for keeping the church open. I found a seven-bedroom rectory with basement let out for brass rubbing, church hall, small flat and basement occupying a substantial portion of prime real estate in the centre of London, all for a couple of services on Sunday, attended by a small congregation. During the rest of the week the church was open for lunchtime concerts, and the occasional society wedding or memorial service.

After three hundred years, this handsome London church, built by Sir Christopher Wren in 1685, had lost its connection to the neighbourhood. In 1980 St James's Church stood marooned on Piccadilly with no recognizable function.

The history of the social significance of relations between church and parish in England, especially in towns and cities, can help explain this loss of connection.

The church and rectory suffered severe bomb damage on the night of 14th October 1940. The Diocese of London had doubts about rebuilding St James's, arguing that any restoration would be a pastiche of Wren's original, and therefore of little historic value. However, Albert Richardson, President of the Royal Academy, across the road on Piccadilly, argued that as a student he had made a detailed study of the church. After the bombing, moulds of all the plasterwork had been made and with four walls still standing the original could be restored faithfully.

Still, officials from the diocese reckoned that the West End of London had enough churches and told parishioners: 'there is always St Martin-in-the-Fields'. Because areas of population growth were demanding new churches elsewhere in England the diocese considered selling this valuable site and using the proceeds to build them. Eventually, due to the persistence of the post-war rector, the War Damage Commission agreed to fund a major part of the reconstruction.

But the connection between church and parish had been lost. The decision to rebuild came too late. St James's Piccadilly was an anachronism.

This had not always been the case. Since the Reformation, parish churches of the Church of England were not just places of worship but had functioned as ecclesiastical town halls. The Vestry Meeting took charge of workhouses, distributing handouts to the poor, paving the roads, disposing of sewage, providing street lighting and keeping the peace. By virtue of its responsibilities in public administration running social services, the parish church became the centre, the focal point of the community.

The Vestry Minutes of St James's reveal two different worlds: one the world of the Establishment at prayer, pews rented out to the Bishop of London, the Archbishop of Canterbury and other bishops, Lord Lieutenants, prime ministers and cabinet ministers, and

Presidents of the Royal College of Surgeons. Literary allusions, like the exchange in Sir John Vanbrugh's *The Relapse*, describe a fashionable church where wealthy aristocratic women came to see and be seen:

Berinthia: Pray which church does your lordship most oblige by his presence?

Foppington: Oh, St James's, Madame: there's much the best company.

Amanda: Is there good preaching too?

Foppington: Why, faith, Madame, I can't tell . . .

Berinthia: You can give us an account of the ladies at least.

Foppington: There is my Lady Tattle, my Lady Pratt, my Lady Titter, my Lady Giggle and my Lady Grin. These sit in the front of the boxes and all church time are the prettiest company in the world, stab my vitals.

This congregation, which, according to parish registers, attended in large numbers, gave St James's the reputation of being a church for the rich, the High Tory Party at prayer. But that was no longer the case at the end of the nineteenth century.

The other world consisted of the poor, the rabble. The Vestry Minutes echo the early writings of Charles Dickens, especially *Oliver Twist* and *Nicholas Nickleby*. Each year the Vestry elected fifty-four watchmen to patrol the streets at night, carrying lanterns. These acted as community police. Six beadles were appointed annually to collect the parish rates and convey to the vestry the names of people eligible for handouts. St James's had its workhouse and a fire engine. It bought horses to help pave the roads. When the cost of bread and flour increased the Vestry urged parishioners to eat potatoes instead. Nineteenth-century minutes complain about 'women of the town' in nearby public houses and large numbers of disorderly people 'roaming around at three o'clock on a Sunday morning'.

The two worlds collided outside St James's on a Sunday. As the rich arrived in their coaches the rabble jeered and the beadles kept them at a distance with staves so the aristocracy would not be polluted by the stench of the mob.

The nineteenth century witnessed widening division between the church's civic and ecclesiastical responsibilities. Rapid urban growth meant that the 'ecclesiastical town hall' could not function as an efficient local authority. In 1894 the Local Government Act removed the Vestry throughout the church from all its administrative responsibilities, thus breaking the historic link between church and its parish. The year 1894 is significant in the decline of the Church of England because its position as the focal point of a community could no longer be assumed. Now it had to be earned.

My job was to create connections between St James's Church with Central London and beyond. Not sure how to set about this I declared at the Induction Service that I would stay for ten years.

First, I had to move fast to address the financial situation. St James's was technically bankrupt with debts of ten thousand pounds. Reserves had been spent. The Brass Rubbing Centre provided the only regular income. The treasurer resigned. Bills for gas and electricity had not been paid for three years. The tiny congregation welcomed me warmly but a sense of desperation was palpable.

'Who is going to boil the eggs?' was the startling question landing in my lap at the first meeting with the church wardens. 'Eggs? What eggs?' St James's had a tradition of two morning services on Sunday, one after the other so the congregation had breakfast in the church hall after the first. Deciding to be accommodating I agreed, took the service, preached, accompanied hymns on the piano (because the organ had broken down, beyond repair) and boiled eggs for the six people who turned up. Two weeks later I cancelled the first service.

Such was the state of affairs at St James's Piccadilly when I arrived in 1980.

This led me to make an important decision: whatever I planned to do I would offer an unqualified, unconditional welcome to everyone. No one would be turned away. This welcome would lead me into much trouble.

To make the point I invented a ritual. At the beginning of any church gathering, worship or meetings as the programme of events and activities began to expand, I appeared with one of the church warden's staves, used by the beadles. One stave, crowned with an attached figure of St James finely carved in silver, had become loose. I told the audience or congregation that they were all welcome and a new dispensation had begun. I indicated this by apparently breaking the stave in two. In fact I simply removed the silver top with a dramatic gesture: the beadles were dismissed. I continued this ritual for some months until someone irritated by my performance arranged for the silver top to be fixed permanently. But the point had been made.

Before starting work I had to make friends with the building and 'welcome myself'. I found the interior intimidating. Its restrained English Baroque interior decorations recreated by Albert Richardson expressed class, privilege and refinement. The furnishings including an exquisitely carved marble font with Adam and Eve, and a wooden reredos with luxuriantly twining vines, birds and creatures by Grinling Gibbons, a contemporary of Wren, were there to be looked at and admired. The building did not receive me. In contrast to Chichester Cathedral of my youth with many dark mysterious spaces where I could hide, St James's was an open public place, flooded with light, cool and rational in its perfect proportions. The church represented a monument to the Age of Enlightenment when Reason defined God.

The night before my induction I locked myself in the church. I lay down on the floor looking up at the ceiling. I lay down in the pews. I danced round the font. I ascended the pulpit and shouted at God, cursing and ordering him to wake up and move in with me. I refused to be beaten and intimidated by the place. At the lectern I aggressively read the genealogies leading up to Christ's birth in St Matthew. I cleared the rubbish from under the altar. Then I perched on it, looking down the church. I whimpered. I shouted.

I was scared. Would the challenge be too much for me? Lying exhausted on the floor I gazed up at the ceiling. Some words from the Gospel came to me: 'Be not afraid.' I fell asleep. On waking I was finally at home.

Next day two coach loads from the St Helier Estate entered a packed church. Though I had told the organizers of the service to put them as near the front as possible they were shunted into the upper gallery to allow dignitaries, the Presidents of the Royal Academy and learned societies, the Master of the Company of Parish Clerks, Peter Brook MP for Westminster, the Mayor of Westminster and clergy to fill the front rows.

We sang 'All my Hope on God is Founded'. The words resonated.

The poet Robert Bridges, drawing on a hymn by Joachim Neander, praises the irreducible nature of God's hope, which remains even when God's trust is betrayed. The hymn ends with a summons to follow:

> Christ doth call
> One and all.
> Ye who follow shall not fall.

Particularly poignant are the words:

> Beauty springeth out of naught.
> Evermore from his store
> New born worlds rise and adore.

Poignant, because the tune to which the hymn is usually sung was written by Herbert Howells shortly after his nine-year-old son, Michael, died suddenly of meningitis in 1935. The director of music at Charterhouse School wrote to the composer inviting him to compose a setting for the hymn. Herbert Howells sat down immediately and wrote. From the depths of his grief the words and music came together, a gift, extraordinary and unexpected. There is nothing like hymn singing to steady the nerves.

I had commissioned a setting of the Beatitudes for the service from the composer Richard Blackford, then a student of the Royal Academy of Music. I started as I intended to continue at St James's, commissioning composers and artists.

The Archdeacon of London placed my hand on the handle of the church door and said: 'By virtue of this mandate I induct you

Donald Reeves into the real and actual possession of this church and benefice of St James's Piccadilly.' I said to myself: 'Thank you. I have already done so.'

After the service I introduced the Bishop of London to my father, who had been driven up from Chichester by my aunt, Anne Heaver, my mother's youngest sister. This turned out to be my father's final visit to London, and he almost didn't make it, saying halfway to London: 'I think we've come far enough!'

My father perked up, shook the bishop's hand and told him: 'He's a good boy really.'

'Does anyone want to say something?' I had just finished a sermon on the Just War. As the British Navy was approaching the Falklands in April 1982 it seemed right to expound theories about the Just War. A congregation of around one hundred and fifty, half being visitors, appeared to be listening. When I stopped and asked the question the attention was palpable. For a moment I stopped being the preacher and as in Beirut and Brasted became once again the teacher. A flood of comments and questions followed: views expressed with passion about invading or not invading the Falklands. Everyone wanted to speak. I made no comment; nor did I attempt to sum up. After twenty minutes I brought the questions to an end. After a pause the congregation rose to say the Creed.

As the congregation left, thanking me, many said: 'That was very brave of you.' These comments indicated a pressing need for opportunities where debate and public conversation could take place in a safe environment, not just at a church service. They reminded me of what I had determined to do on my arrival in November 1980. Still not clear as to how to 'raise the questions', I wanted to create opportunities for this to happen, to reclaim the idea of 'the public'.

Just before starting work, I visited Washington, DC. I had been invited to meet the members of an evangelical, ecumenical church: the Church of the Saviour. There I met Rustum Roy, a distinguished metallurgy scientist and also a radical Christian, who asked me the question: 'What are you going to do to stop a Third World War?'

He added: 'You should take advantage of St James's Piccadilly as a prestigious location near Whitehall and Westminster.'

His words were timely. Fear of a global nuclear war reached a peak in the early 1980s. The West perceived the Soviet Union as belligerent and unpredictable. SS20 missiles deployed by the Russians were targeted on cities in Western Europe. NATO planned a new generation of Pershing and cruise missiles, some to be sited in Britain.

Margaret Thatcher, now prime minister, relished her image as 'the iron lady', bestowed by the Soviet Union in 1986 after her speech warning that the Russians were intent on world domination and had the means to achieve it. Paranoia and demonizing of the Soviet Union were stoked by the prime minister's hectoring and confrontational style. The prime minister might have been less enthusiastic about her image as the iron lady if she had known what it meant. The Russians were referring to the 'iron maiden', a medieval instrument of torture and death, widespread in Eastern Europe, consisting of a metal coffin carved on the outside in the form of a woman. Sharp spikes were fixed to the interior of the lid. Victims would be bound, thrown inside and slowly impaled as the lid shut on them. The Russians were commenting on Margaret Thatcher's lethal belligerence. And the president of the world's most powerful country, the USA, stood side by side with her defending freedom.

I got a taste of this paranoia in September 1984 as member of a delegation from the British Council of Churches visiting the Soviet Union. Channel 4 asked me to do a five-minute comment before I left for Moscow. My anodyne piece about 'wanting to discover the humanity of the Russian people' provoked a stream of abuse: 'A man of the cloth should not be allowed on television to give a party political broadcast on behalf of the communist party.' 'The Rev Donald Reeves stated he will be visiting Russia soon. Then I suggest he should stay there.'

Rusty Roy's question to me demanded an active response. He posed the same question to a mutual friend, Neil Wates.

Neil Wates was Chairman of Wates Building Company. I met him through friends of Mervyn Stockwood. He became the first of several highly significant benefactors and colleagues in my life.

From our first meeting Neil warmed to my enthusiastic plans for transplanting my Chicago experience to London.

A successful businessman, he was prepared to take risks supporting the work of pioneers. Neil paid for all the administrative back-up I needed at St Peter's and helped me establish the Urban Ministry Project. As boss of a major company he could be intimidating and overpowering, but I drew inspiration from his unfaltering commitment and passion for justice and peace.

Neil died of a rare form of cancer in 1985, in the prime of life. I had never known him well; but I missed his unflinching support and encouragement, even when I made mistakes. He remains an example to people with resources and influence. Today, with regrettably too few exceptions, the wealthy prefer to support only those charities with a successful track record. Before they donate, enquiries are set up to examine the charities' targets and outcomes. Risk-free delivery is the key concept. If targets cannot be safely delivered, donors will look elsewhere. This practice is a form of narcissism: the rich donor can announce: 'Look at me supporting this good work. See how the concrete results promote my corporate image as a caring organization.'

Neil liked to be directly involved in the work he supported. He preached at St Peter's. We had long discussions in the vicarage study, working out concepts of liturgical celebration that were emerging at church services. An eavesdropper would have been hard put to identify him as a donor. We both learned as we went along. Today how do people with Neil's resources and influence learn anything when they are protected by the circumstances of their position, by chauffeurs, personal assistants and their company foundations?

Neil and I considered Rusty Roy's question to both of us: 'What are you going to do to stop a Third World War?' and agreed to establish an organization for diplomatic dialogue on military and political issues and named it Dunamis. *Dunamis* is the Greek word for power, capability and influence. We put together a group whose common concerns were the nuclear threat, global injustice and environmental degradation. Mark Collier, a former Dominican monk, had experience of reconciliation and development in South Africa and Zimbabwe. Neil's wife, Jenifer Wates, had concerns around matters of public policy. Neil was committed to connect the world of politics with spiritual values. My contribution as rector consisted of sustaining Dunamis as a forum where debates, lectures, seminars and public conversations could take place.

Dunamis provided a safe public arena in which people of widely different views could consider critical issues of international and personal security in a calm constructive spirit. We hoped this would help reduce polarization in the world and produce a more thought-ful and non-confrontational model. We functioned in public with lectures and debates taking place in the church itself; and in private in the rectory with suppers for small groups of specially invited peo-ple from different sides. These private meetings were not publicized. Discreetly and skilfully chaired, they enabled opponents to explore each other's positions and motives and to invite second thoughts.

We appointed Ronald Higgins as Director of Dunamis. An expe-rienced and respected diplomat he brought to St James's many of the leading protagonists in defence, international politics, political phi-losophy and ethics as well as specialists in environmental and devel-opmental matters. He administered Dunamis for fifteen years.

In that time people of the quality and experience of Denis Hea-ley, David Owens, Professors Michael Howard, Geoffrey Best, Ber-nard Williams, Lawrence Freedman, Sir Frank Roberts, Richard Luce, Merlyn Rees, Lord Gladwyn, Adam Roberts, Dr Anthony Storr, Field Marshall Lord Carver, Joseph Rotblat, Generals Beach, Turze and Younger, John Biffen, Julian Critchley, Clive Ponting, Bruce Kent, Sonny Ramphal, Bishop Trevor Huddleston, Gra-ham Leonard, Michael Hare Duke, Mark Santer, John Robinson, Lord Judd, Mary Kaldor, Tony Benn, Mohammad Sulima and Jung Chang (before *Wild Swans* made her famous), among others, came to speak in public and discuss in private.

Establishment figures who vigorously opposed the then flourish-ing Campaign for Nuclear Disarmament (CND) were able to meet its leaders. American and Chinese officials could unbend without, in Ronald Higgins's words, 'ping pong as mediator'. Peace workers discussed policy issues with generals, and both with representatives from the Soviet Embassy.

Dunamis did not prevent a Third World War. But we believed that opponents could learn from each other; and that in the highly dangerous period of the early 1980s we created opportunities for conversation and discussion that helped many of the most passionately opinionated of opinion formers to think again. As Neil Wates often reminded us, we managed to plant 'subversives in place'.

Twenty years later Ronald's patience, perseverance and skill were an inspiration for my work in conflict transformation in the Balkans.

Dunamis was unique. While organizations like Chatham House, a few yards from St James's, and the Institute of Strategic Studies had similar concerns, they were closed institutions. The public face of Dunamis prevented the conversations from becoming too elitist. The stream of people prepared to speak and discuss at St James's over fifteen years proved Dunamis to be more than a moment of fitful idealism.

Dunamis methods went against the grain and it had many detractors. In *One of Us*, Hugo Young's biography of Margaret Thatcher, a Foreign Office official who admired her more than most is quoted as saying that 'she doesn't think in the supple way of someone who is occupied with foreign affairs a lot of the time'. Negotiation was not her style. When she appointed Sir Anthony Parsons, Britain's ambassador to the UN, to be her foreign policy adviser he told her: 'But Prime Minister, I must remind you that I am a member of the Foreign Office.' 'I know, I know,' she said, 'But I don't consider *you* to be one of *them!*'[1] Dunamis with an experienced former diplomat in charge was considered 'one of *them*'.

Dunamis also had its base in an Anglican church, one which used to have a reputation for establishment connections. Five of my predecessors became Archbishops of Canterbury; two bishops, three deans, three archdeacons and numerous prebendaries. Now the media perceived St James's as 'a load of lefties'.

Anyone from the tiny minority criticizing the Falklands War was branded a traitor in a country whipped up by the tabloids and the prime minister into a patriotic frenzy. 'Rejoice! Rejoice!' commanded Margaret Thatcher on the re-taking of the tiny island of South Georgia, an important staging post to the Antarctic and its mineral resources. 'Gotcha!' screamed the *Sun* headline on the sinking of the Argentinian battleship *Belgrano*. Britain saw itself defending the last fragment of empire, and the prime minister's belligerence recalled Churchill, the hero of the Second World War. Few dared question the purpose and worth of the war. Repelled by this jingoism I joined the anti-war rally in Hyde Park. Twenty years later massive demonstrations attempted to stop the invasion of Iraq, but in 1982 only a few people gathered to protest against the re-taking of some small islands on the other side of the world.

One Sunday afternoon I was invited to share the platform in Hyde Park with Tony Benn, Mick McGahey, a former communist trade union leader, and other speakers. The media were curious about my presence: what was this priest doing up there on the platform? Next day on Piccadilly a thin-faced man in a bowler hat and carrying an umbrella stopped me. He brought his face close to mine and spat: 'You should be shot. You are a traitor.'

I met Margaret Thatcher once. President Kaunda of Zambia on a state visit to England had invited me to a banquet held by the Zambians. Colin Morris, Head of BBC Religious Broadcasting and friend of Kenneth Kaunda, proposed that since the president was a preacher, the BBC should televise a Eucharist from St James's Piccadilly on the last Sunday of his visit, which is how I got to meet him.

Claridges Hotel hosted the banquet in a room that reminded me of the church hall at St Peter's, all grey walls and garish Exit signs. After an hour of desultory conversation and speeches, President Kaunda stood up with his entourage and loudly sang the African Freedom Song. After a pause waiters served coffee and people began to mingle. I noticed a back door where I hoped to slip out unnoticed. Turning to leave I stepped backwards and on to someone's shoes. It turned out to be the prime minister's. She immediately apologized for not attending the Sunday service with Kaunda, explaining that on the last Sunday of every month her church near Chequers had a parade of scouts and guides 'and we never miss it'. That she knew who I was surprised me. We talked for a while about the British Council. Her government had just announced cuts. But Margaret Thatcher listened to me intently.

Then suddenly the Queen advanced towards us. I stood for a few moments between the two women. 'Why didn't the Church do something?' the Queen wanted to know, looking at me challengingly. She was referring to the pause after the Zambian's freedom song. 'The Church should have sung something,' declared the Queen. The prime minister said: 'We should have sung Rule Britannia!' 'Jerusalem would have been better,' countered the Queen. The two women stared for a moment at each other, the Queen revealing sparkling white teeth before walking away.

Queen Elizabeth the Queen Mother, who someone informed me used to attend St James's, accepted my invitation to be guest of honour at the three hundredth anniversary of the consecration of the church on 13th July 1984. 'As a little girl,' she told me, 'I used to come here when Mr Temple was rector.' She was referring to William Temple, later to become Archbishop of Canterbury. 'But I never understood a word he said.'

The Bishop of London, Graham Leonard, preached at the service.

Something needs to be said about my relationship with him. When Bishop Ellison, who had chosen me to be rector, retired in Easter 1981, many hoped that John Habgood, then Bishop of Durham, would follow him as next Bishop of London. Two names were sent to the Prime Minister, Margaret Thatcher: John Habgood, the favourite, and in second place Graham Leonard, Bishop of Truro. The prime minister resisted pressure not to appoint Graham Leonard, whose conservative views on the ordination of women priests and the relationship between Methodism and the Church of England were considered too divisive for such a senior position. But she had the constitutional right to chose whoever she wanted, even though Graham Leonard had been the Church's second choice.

When I attended his enthronement as the 130th Bishop of London at St Paul's Cathedral on 21st September 1981, I listened with apprehension as they placed him on the throne, according to the rubric: 'causes him to be seated', with the blessing 'that mounting this day to Episcopal Throne he may ever be a worthy ruler of thy Church and people'.

I had good reason to be worried because as my unqualified welcome to everyone began to blossom in a range of activities to be described later, complaints were frequently made to the bishop about the 'red parson of Piccadilly' and the presence of the New

My mother, 1936

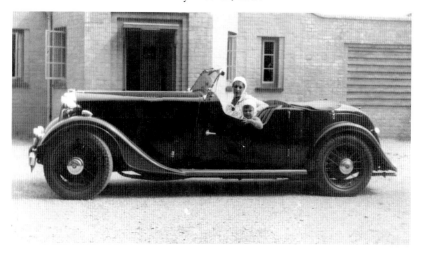

With my mother in the Lagonda

Off to preparatory school

My father's garage bombed by the Germans – 10 February 1943

National Service – 2nd Lieutenant. (Donald Reeves top row, one from the right)

Ordination. (Donald Reeves third from the right)

Getting close to Michael Ramsey

The parish priest at Piccadilly

With Dr Kenneth Kaunda

Meeting Pope John Paul II - Banja Luka, 22 June 2003

Press Conference Banja Luka

Immersed in J.S. Bach

Age project which we hosted. I never saw copies of these letters to the bishop, nor his replies.

He summoned me regularly to his office and I got used to the walk from Piccadilly to London House off Smith Square, finding refreshment in St James's Park as I observed the ducklings, baby geese and other birds swimming around. Over the years I observed Downing Street turning into a fortress. One day to my surprise the lake had been drained for cleaning and I noticed that it was only inches deep.

The bishop always received me kindly but the meetings were unsatisfactory. He could not deflect me from my ministry, but despite our different views, I still needed his reassurance. This never happened, so I remained unsure where I stood with him, and we both avoided discussing the matter directly. However, we remained on good terms. He never criticized me publicly and helped generously when I asked for money to give to people in need.

Graham Leonard disliked the ostentation that went with being a prelate. Although he held an exalted view of the priesthood and the episcopate, being a priest and bishop was so much part of his being that he did not need the trappings of office to prove it. He accepted my invitation to celebrate Holy Communion at 8.30 in the morning before the main anniversary service at 11.00, and having warned me he would be delayed said: 'You start, and I'll take over when I get there.' Twenty minutes late he half ran in calling out: 'It's all right, I'm here!'

However, Graham Leonard was an unpopular Bishop of London.

Trevor Beeson writes how 'Leonard appeared to have been quite unmoved by the controversy' (over his appointment as Bishop of London), and adds: 'when soon after his retirement he became a

Roman Catholic this occasioned neither surprise nor regret in his own Church'.[2]

I had drawn up a service of carefully chosen hymns, readings and prayers for the Anniversary Celebration.

Hymns describe our place in the world. We sang 'Praise to the Lord, the Almighty, King of Creation'. Many women and some men in the congregation objected to the language of patriarchy and male domination. Normally I avoided choosing such hymns because of the strong feelings they generated. I defended the choice of this hymn for this occasion and explained by way of mitigation that these and other Reformation hymns had been translated by Catherine Winkworth, who had been active in promoting women's rights to university education while she lived in Bristol at the end of the nineteenth century. Her translations matched the sentiments of praise and thanksgiving expressed in the confident melodies of the Lutheran German choral tradition.

Catherine Winkworth's memorial is in Bristol Cathedral. It says her rendering into English verse of 'the treasures of German sacred poetry opened a new source of light, consolation and strength in many thousand homes'.

Bearing in mind the substantial number of agnostics in the congregation that day, for no one wanted to miss out on a royal occasion, I also chose a hymn by Frederick Hosmer, an American Unitarian. This hymn has played a significant part of my life because of its hope and trust in God when:

> All wrongs stands revealed
> When justice shall be throned in might
> And every hurt be healed.

Generally I relate more easily to Machiavelli's realism in his under-standing of human nature, that nations are always preparing for the next war, than to this utopian vision of peace. But I am inspired by this hymn which urges action with a quality of trust, tenacity and endurance:

> But the slow watches of the night
> Not less to God belong;
> And for the everlasting right
> The silent stars are strong.

The words are enhanced by being set to a traditional Irish folk mel-ody, which appeared in many guises, most unexpectedly as the tune to a Jacobite satire on Scottish Presbyterianism, telling of the hang-ing of a cat for catching a mouse on the Sabbath. No one knows who brought Hosmer's words together with this music when it first appeared in one of the monumental achievements of the Church of England: *Hymns Ancient and Modern*, first published in 1861.

The muted service, framing an incomprehensible sermon by the Bishop of London on the 'cosmic Christ', was happily enlivened by Bach, Vivaldi and Handel sparklingly performed by the St James's Baroque Players, founded and conducted by Ivor Bolton, the Direc-tor of Music.[3] The orchestra became the mainstay of the Lufthansa Festival of Baroque Music, which kept St James's as its base for many years.

The service opened the fourth Piccadilly Festival of Arts, includ-ing exhibitions, concerts and films. Steve Bell, a political cartoon-ist, had generously donated a selection of his work to the festival, specifying that any profits of sale should go to the Greenham Com-mon women demonstrating against American nuclear missiles based there. At that time these women represented the forefront of radical political activity. The cartoons, including a wittily scurrilous depiction of the Royal Family, hung in the rectory where the Queen Mother was entertained after the celebration with a gin and Dubonnet cocktail (described with precision over the phone by her equerry, anxious we got the proportions exactly right). Should we remove the cartoon that might cause offence? In the event she never noticed. Instead she kept looking with alarm at the un-ticking grandfather clock in need of repair on the landing with fingers permanently fixed at the moment of her arrival, and probably wondered why time stood still.

Nervous about the visit I had forgotten to clean my shoes so kept my feet hidden as much as possible under my cassock. The Queen Mother talked about nothing in particular for twenty minutes, and enjoyed the attention of Mackerel and Tyger, the rectory cats. Apart from the well-honed expertise of making conversation, a skill shared with her daughter, she had another proficiency: climbing in and out of cars nimbly and with an elegance rarely seen in an octogenarian. As she sat down in her car ready to leave, announcing she was giving lunch to some Spaniards, she paused gravely and gave me a direct look for the first time, saying: 'I know what you are doing here. Thank you!'

I met the Queen Mother one more time at St James's when she attended a family wedding. She said afterwards: 'How nice to come to a proper wedding!'

Princess Margaret, who was accompanying her turned to me and asked: 'How many Muslims have you converted?'

By the time of the Queen Mother's attendance at the Tercentenary the church was no longer the best kept secret in London.

Funds were raised for a public relations company to promote our programmes of activities, to promote St James's as a 'living church which offers a ministry relevant to the spiritual needs of our time', and 'the establishment of St James's as an exciting accessible resource in the heart of London, offering facilities for a whole range of activities and events both sacred and secular'. We created a brand to attract attention in a competitive market, for different groups, different congregations, and different audiences who could say: 'yes, St James's Piccadilly is my spiritual home'. By the end of the 1980s Dot Cotton told Pauline Fowler in *EastEnders* that she intended to celebrate Christmas Eve at St James's Piccadilly.

Within four years the parish room where I boiled the eggs for the Sunday morning congregation had been converted into a restaurant. The Piccadilly Arts and Film Festival and the Lufthansa Festival of Baroque Music were established fixtures on the London entertainment scene. Alongside the Dunamis project I set up lunch time and evening lecture series that continued for the rest of my time at Piccadilly, culminating in May 1997 with a verbal punch-up between the present Bishop of Durham, Tom Wright, then Dean of Lichfield, and AN Wilson about the true founder of Christianity: Jesus or Paul? There was standing room only. Some of the lecture series were published. *Prejudice in Religion* raised the question: Can we move beyond it? *Church and State* examined the idea of disestablishment of the Church of England. 'Getting political in Piccadilly', the *Evening Standard* headlined.

Mother Teresa attended our first major event in July 1981. She came to dedicate the Prayer for Peace in London.

A retinue of five sisters escorted Mother Teresa, who had arrived early, into my study and then left. Mackerel and Tyger sat quietly in front of her and watched unwaveringly while we spoke.

I offered coffee or tea. 'No, just some water.' She took the glass in her hands, paused, made the sign of the cross and drank, the cats staring.

We spoke little and she did not seem interested in anything I had to say. So I shut up and we remained silent for several minutes.

In a packed church I spotted the journalist Richard Ingrams, who occasionally excoriated me in *Private Eye*. After dedicating the Prayer for Peace, Mother Teresa answered questions from the congregation and became agitated on the subject of abortion. I brought the event to an end and the five nuns swept the tiny figure of Mother Teresa away to her next appointment.

We had logistical problems concerning the Prayer for Peace, finding a place in the crowded rectory, already filling up with offices. A friend wished to dispose of a caravan, but it was illegal to have a vehicle on church premises. We collected it and four of us waited till the early hours of the morning when Piccadilly emptied of traffic for a brief period then pushed the caravan across the road and down the steps into the courtyard. It remained for some years and was then replaced.

The caravan did a brisk trade in selling the Prayer for Peace. Then in 1982 it opened as a Help and Advice Centre, evolving into a counselling service, open seven days a week and staffed by twenty-one volunteer students from the Centre for Counselling and Psychotherapy Education. Over a period of twenty years about twenty-five thousand people have knocked on the caravan door as a point of first contact for those seeking help.

This seemed to me to be a more productive use of the caravan.

Although the Prayer for Peace sold well in the first months, I could never recite it with conviction. No one could disagree with the sentiments, but the words were vapid and limp:

> Lead me from death to life,
> From falsehood to truth,
> Lead me from despair to hope,
> From fear to trust.
> Lead from hate to love,
> From war to peace.
> Let peace fill our hearts,
> Our world, our universe.

At least it should have been 'lead us' not 'lead me'. I remember thinking at the time that Margaret Thatcher and Arthur Scargill would have had quite different ideas about peace.

Those early years at St James's, beginning with the visit of Mother Teresa, set the pattern. Alongside the projects carrying on their work, I welcomed major world figures: Dr Sochitsu Sen presented the Japanese Tea Ceremony at the time of the Great Japan Exhibition in 1981. Father Roger Schutz, the Prior of Taizé, and forty Taizé brothers celebrated a watch-night service on 30th December in a church packed with young people.

Then I invited the women demonstrating at Greenham Common to make St James's their London base. In 1984 during the epic struggle between the miners and the government, St James's provided a base for the miner's wives to rest in between money-raising activities. Walking down Piccadilly with Michael Foot, then leader

of the Labour Party, he saw a banner on the church railings supporting the miners and turning to me said: 'If you go on like this you'll
make a Christian of me yet!'

Peter Jay, a former ambassador to Washington and then financial
journalist at the BBC, attended a service anointing a young man
dying from AIDS and told me: 'I like what you have done here,
making St James's Piccadilly a part of London again.'

In 1984 I invited Henri Nouwen to undertake a teaching mission
to a new and growing congregation attracted by the variety of programmes which were on offer, and the welcome we gave. A Catholic priest, Henri Nouwen had taught at Yale and Harvard and was
regarded as one of the most influential spiritual teachers of the
twentieth century.

He could not accept my invitation, but came to visit me and
explain why it had come too late. He had had enough of speaking
to large groups and planned to join the L'Arche community called
Daybreak, in Canada near Toronto. These communities care for
people with lifelong impairments and disabilities. 'I want to live
with people who would value me for what I am,' he told me, 'and
who would not be impressed by my books or teaching, because my
friends there can neither read nor write.'

'How do you pray?' he asked me the moment he arrived and sat
down. This was a direct question, not in the least aggressive. 'It is
difficult,' I replied. 'I am like a juggler and I have to keep all the balls
in the air, and all the time new balls arrive. But this is how I like it. I
appreciate retreats at monasteries when I can. There I don't have to
do anything, just look out of the window. That is easy for me to do.
Most of my praying is thanking God and saying: "over to you".'

Henri Nouwen asked how I coped with fatigue after major religious events, such as Holy Week and Easter, which had just passed. He continued: 'Do you know the story in St Luke's Gospel when an unclean spirit comes out of someone and wanders over the desert looking for a resting place? Finding nowhere, he says: "I will return to the home I left." He finds the home clean and tidy. The unclean spirit gathers seven demons and they enter and settle there, so that person's situation is worse than before.'

I knew exactly what he meant. He told me that he felt most vulnerable after speaking engagements, and therefore could be more easily taken advantage of. I told him how I found it easy to be lazy, probably inherited from my father, adding how I enjoyed watching rubbish on TV.

Later I came across his impression of our meeting in his book *The Road to Daybreak*:

This afternoon I visited Donald Reeves, the pastor of St James's Anglican Church in Piccadilly.

Donald Reeves is a man of many gifts. He is an activist, a contemplative, a social worker, an artist, a caring pastor, a restless mover, a visionary and a pragmatist. In five years he converted a practically lifeless downtown Anglican parish into a vibrant centre of prayer and action. When I arrived at the rectory I could sense the vibrancy of the place. Within a few minutes I had met a bishop, a Jew, an ex-convict, an artist and an administrator. Donald introduced them all to me with words of praise and encouragement. You could sense that people were doing new things here, things they believed in. The parish is a place for meditation, counselling, art events, concerts, peace making, book publishing and hospitality. It is a place that welcomes traditional Christians as well as people who feel alienated from the Church. It is an incredibly diverse place, embracing charismatics as well as activists, Christians as well as non-Christians.

Listening to Donald I realized how much he had been influenced by new communities in the United States, especially the Sojourners' Fellowship and the Church of the Savior in Washington, DC. I felt invigorated just being with him and walking around the place with him.

As I left, Donald gave me some of his writings. On the cover of his 'ten year plan' for the church he wrote:

> A vision without a task is a dream;
> A task without a vision is drudgery;
> A vision and a task is the hope of the world.

Nothing better can sum up the spirit of St James's Piccadilly than these words.[4]

Vision. Task. Hope. What is this vision and task? Apart from creating a community centre in central London I had to communicate this vision.

Although three books were published while I was in Piccadilly and I made eight films for the BBC on *Making Sense of Religion*, and took part in radio and TV programmes, I saw the sermon as the means to convey what I had to say.

At St Peter's Morden I had felt restless in the pulpit. I needed to move about, be in closer contact with the congregation, not above them.

So the pulpit was abandoned and I stood at a lectern in the front of the first pews. There I could look directly at people, catch their eye. Moving about enabled me to hold people's attention. This was necessary because I needed time; time to lay out what I wanted to say. Quarter of an hour; twenty minutes were not sufficient. Forty minutes too long; the pews became uncomfortable. Therefore as I moved around I could sense when the attention span of my listeners wavered, and would lighten the tone, vary the mood with stories, personal interjections, questions. The best sermons evoked the response: 'We could hear you thinking.'

At Cuddesdon I had been taught to write out the sermon and then to read it. A theatre director told me that when a preacher reading the sermon looks up momentarily and then looks down, searching for the words, the listeners' attention is loosened; the thread has gone. So sermons can seem very long. As Lionel Blue tells it: a rabbi preaches a long sermon. After a while a man in the congregation leaves the synagogue and returns when the sermon is finished. 'Why did you leave?' asks the rabbi. 'I went to get a haircut,' says the man. 'Why didn't you get one before?' asks the rabbi. 'I didn't need one then,' says the man.

The stand-up does not need a script. I reduced the text to notes, then I discarded the script altogether.

Sermon preparation could take a week, even longer. In between my other activities I would mull over the Biblical text. By the time of the sermon I knew exactly what I was going to say.

I encountered two hazards when preaching free of the text. At times I became unnecessarily provocative, making cheap political points which raised a laugh but were a diversion from my theme. The second and more serious hazard concerned my increasing eloquence so that sometimes the congregation would respond with applause or the occasional hallelujah: more oratory than preaching. I received letters and comments which indicated that my sermons were becoming entertainment. So my style of preaching was in danger of reinforcing the very infantilism I had observed in Morden and Maidstone.

A consequence of these hazards, combined with the physical nature of the liturgy, which involved much embracing during the Peace at the Eucharist, meant that a number of people in the congregation, some quite disturbed, transferred their thoughts, feelings and desires on to me. This transference is a familiar stage in psychotherapy, a useful tool for the therapist. But I was a preacher, not a psychotherapist. I had difficulty handling this transference. I was both loved and hated. Therefore I resisted the temptation to be over-rhetorical and too eloquent, but continued preaching without the text or even notes.

Not all my sermons were solo efforts. Occasionally I continued the practice begun during the Falklands War of inviting anyone to say anything they wished. This meant I did not always have the last word. As much as possible I resisted the urge to 'sum up' and bring the sermon to a neatly wrapped positive conclusion.

Preaching is a performance; not in the histrionic sense or as a piece of theatre but as an interpreter.

Dame Gillian Weir, one of the world's finest concert organists, said in a lecture, Aspects of Vision, in May 1999: 'We must be true to the composer . . . we must also be certain that we are being true to our understanding of the piece.'[5] So she urges the player to learn the context of each piece: the style, the instruments used by the composer, and then not just to reproduce a mechanical repetition of notes, but to bring his or her own imagination to the performance. 'It is only when the player's instincts bond with the soul of the work itself that the performance becomes an interpretation.' The final piece of the puzzle is the audience. Gillian Weir describes how on occasion a bond develops between the music, the performer and the listener so that at the conclusion of the music the work as a whole 'hangs in the air', before dissolving into silence.

The preacher's art is similar. I worked on the Biblical text and then laid it aside, bringing my own questions to the words. The Bible does not just address the reader; we bring our questions and then as the sermon unfolds it may be that a bond between preacher and congregation is created so as it is brought to an end (including comments and interjections) there is a palpable silence, the words like the musical notes hanging in the air before they too dissolve. Preaching like music begins and ends in silence.

It does not always happen like that. Regularly an elderly man stood up to ask: 'When is the New Jerusalem coming?' I got used to seeing him about to interrupt and would tell the congregation: 'I know we are going to be asked about the New Jerusalem.' 'That's right,' he would say, 'when is it coming?' 'I don't know,' I would reply. He seemed satisfied with my answer.

Once I told a neighbouring priest in London: 'I always preach as if this is my last sermon.' 'That's a bit much,' he said. 'No,' I told him. 'This moment is our opportunity and we should use it well.'

Two Americans from Alabama visited St James's and as they left they said to me: 'You sound like a Southern Baptist. Different message!'

An artist stands in front of a blank canvas. Before the first brush-stroke there is a moment of concentration: focusing on the source from which this new creation will be fashioned.

I know what it is to stand in front of a blank canvas: in this case an empty space in a church in the centre of London. As I have described, this canvas began to fill up: St James's began to take an active part in the life of London.

Among all these activities I came across a road block: the way ahead was unclear. I needed to discover that source of inspiration which would release whatever creativity I had. If God is that source, then what sort of God?

My experience in Chicago and Morden drew me towards the left, but the tone of my preaching and writing resonated across the political spectrum.

During the Urban Ministry Project's survey we used the language of sociology and politics rather than religion. It was easier that way: less embarrassing. I was nervous then of appearing irrelevant and sounding silly. Of course theological reflection was encouraged, but it rarely happened.

If the Christian language is reduced to a footnote, then Christianity itself becomes little more than an archaic residue.

So the problem remains: how to speak of God in a public way in a culture which was largely indifferent to the Church and Christianity.

The document I gave Henri Nouwen from which he quoted was 'A Plan for Ten Years for St James's', which had a distribution well into five figures. I wrote it using deliberately as little Christian language as possible because I wanted to engage all readers' interest so they would not be put off by churchiness. I wrote of a new community which I hoped would emerge, drawing on the philosopher Ernst Friedrich Schumacher's dictum: 'small is beautiful'. This is what he wrote:

I think we can see the conflict of attitudes which will decide our future. On the one hand I see the people who think they can cope with our economic, technological crisis by the methods current, only more so – the people of the forward stampede. On the other side there are people in search of a new life style who seek to return to basic truths about man and his world. I call them home comers. The term 'home comer' has a religious connotation. It takes a good deal of courage to say 'No' to the fashion, and fascination of the age, and to question the presupposition of a civilization which appears to conquer the world. The requisite strength can only be derived from deep conviction.[6]

Those 'basic truths' or 'deep convictions' were not described. I wrote how churches should remember 'whose they are, and where they come from, and thus being called to become communities of loving defiance'.

The 'journey inward' and 'communal remembering and celebrating the vision in the liturgy' were described. However, it was altogether short on detail. For new work, new thinking, detail is all important.

Looking to the right, to the conservative evangelicals starting to flex their muscles, I could not find a home with them. Their God was too domesticated, suitable for their own certainties. Nor did I feel comfortable with their mantra: 'the authority of the scriptures'. I wondered how many evangelicals had read the sixty-six books of the Bible, not just a few selected texts. If they had they would have noticed for a start that the Old Testament God, though faithful to Israel and his people, was variously irascible, deaf, elusive, sleepily indifferent, impatient and prone to violence.

I looked to the Church of England, to its history since my ordination: a story of unchecked steady decline both in numbers and in significance. In spite of the excitement generated by South Bank religion, the formidable spiritual and intellectual leadership of Michael Ramsey, Archbishop of Canterbury, initiatives in revising the prayer book, new forms of training for priests and much else, I found nothing inspirational to help me discover the focus of that canvas.

Then in 1978 a small book, some hundred and fifty pages, appeared. Its publication helped to shape eighteen years of my preaching and teaching. *The Prophetic Imagination* by Walter Brueggemann, Professor of Old Testament at Columbia Theological Seminar in Decatur, Georgia USA, followed by a stream of articles and books, helped me to lay the foundations of a radical Christian counter-culture.[7]

Walter Brueggemann's compelling analysis of American culture and society has become ever more relevant over the years. He describes how 'the dominant scripting of both selves and communities in our society, for both liberals and conservatives, is the script of therapeutic, technological, consumer militarism that permeates every dimension of our common life.'[8]

By 'therapeutic' he means the assumption that there is a product available to counteract every discomfort so life can be lived pain-free.

By 'technological' he refers to the assumption that every problem can be fixed.

By 'consumerism' he refers to the assumption of our right to happiness that can be found through buying, getting, having and consuming without regard to neighbours or to the planet. The incentive to get rich is regarded as intrinsic to human nature.

In the public imagination, expressed especially in the tabloid press, role models are now the celebrities, fat cats and big spenders with their opulent lifestyles: mansions, yachts, jewels and private jets. They live apart from the rest of the world, erecting razor wire fences, their properties patrolled by guards and dogs.

Added to this is the pervasive and expensive militarism, together with a flourishing arms trade whose purpose is to protect those 'freedoms' of a therapeutic, technological and consumerist society. The reasoning is: if we are safe, we shall be happy.

Walter Brueggemann places alongside this analysis the prophetic traditions of the Old Testament and the ministry of Jesus. It is rare to find an academic theologian who writes with such elegance, passion and compassion. Not only does he respect the Bible, he loves it and frequently quotes the verse from Psalm 119: 'Lucerna pedibus meis – thy word is a lantern unto my feet, and a light unto my paths.' It could be said of Walter Brueggemann himself some verses later: 'Thy testimonies have I claimed as mine heritage for ever: and why? They are the very joy of my heart . . . I have applied my heart to fulfil thy statutes alway, even unto the end.'

His analysis resonated in the Britain in the 1980s and 1990s.

It was a happy coincidence that 'prophetic' was placed next to 'imagination'.

The 'imagination' is moral, not in the sense of moralistic, but as conveying the idea of an epic journey to new horizons, always just beyond reach. Imagination is neither fantasy nor daydreaming. Imagination is the capacity to give birth to something new which changes the way we live. It refuses to renege on the responsibility to 'the other'. The face of 'the other' invites and demands an unconditional response. 'Where are you?' comes the question. 'Here am I; here we are' comes the response.

Within a Christian context the imagination is fuelled by the prophets, and the writers of the Wisdom Literature: Psalms, Proverbs and the Book of Job, and the Gospels.

I rapidly embraced their insights: they were partly present already and I scurried back to the Bible, ransacking it to discover what I had been missing. I will show what happens when the prophetic imagination is taken seriously.

But first I wanted to draw attention to the Bible. In May 1985 we arranged a reading of the entire Authorized Version without pause, the first time such a marathon reading (a Biblethon) had taken place anywhere, although there have been other readings since. It took ninety-nine hours and a team of three hundred and fifty readers, some well known, most unknown. These included religious and political leaders of every faith and party, the jobless and homeless, stars of sport and entertainment, office cleaners and policemen, men, women and children from every walk of life.

Some listeners brought sleeping bags and slept in the pews. Others came and then returned. The readers had taken considerable care in their preparation, particularly in pronouncing the names of Old Testament characters correctly.

Everyone who came appreciated the opportunity to hear the whole Bible read rather than a few chosen verses. The Biblethon ended with Roger Rees, then starring in the Royal Shakespeare Company's production of *Nicholas Nickleby*, reciting the Book of Revelation. Far from exhaustion there was a palpable sense of excitement and tension as the reading ended with the words:

> He which testifieth these things saith
> Surely I come quickly. Amen. Even so,

Come Lord Jesus. The grace of our Lord
Jesus Christ be with you All. Amen.

Then we sang one of Catherine Winkworth's most inspired translations from the *Lyrica Germanica*: 'Now thank we all our God'.

The reading of the Bible placed the book firmly in the public eye and in the consciousness of the congregation. But how then does the prophetic imagination address our present culture as Walter Brueggemann describes it?

The answer is: with difficulty – because of the extent to which Christians of all kinds, liberal and conservative, had assimilated those assumptions I have just described, assumptions experienced as unalterable facts. That is the way things are, it is said, and always will be. This forgets that what we have assembled can also be dismantled.

Meanwhile 'Anything goes at St James's', people from the outside said frequently, and a bishop told me: 'People like you just make it up as you go along!'

This record needs to be put straight.

Here follows the briefest sketch of the themes explored over eighteen years.

Inevitably the questioning which I have described creates unease. It was as if a community of exiles was coming into being. Most of the Old Testament was collated at a time when the Jewish community had been exiled to Babylon. The New Testament was written out of the experience of a community marginalized in an all-powerful oppressive Roman Empire.

Exile provokes a sense of the absence of God, frequently described in the Psalms of complaint, and specifically in the Book of Lamentation. Sometimes some of us tried to write lamentations for our own time, not least on the destruction of the environment, but these read like geography lessons; our efforts were forced and prosaic.

We needed to write like the poet from Sarajevo mourning the destruction of her city:

> In the City, those still living
> Reject the consolation of history
> Where everything gets repeated.
> The City watches sadly
> The freshly drawn omens of destiny
> Unplanned new graveyards
> Wherever the heart had trod
> Having come from its infernal darkness.
> What is the destiny of the wounded City?[9]

Exiles also recall the deepest memories – easier said than done because amnesia is powerful, especially when culture is organized against history and only 'the now' has significance. Hence a demand for instant comprehension, instant explanation and instant clarity: the sound bite.

I experienced this demand regularly on chat shows and discussion programmes. Once the garrulous presenter Janet Street-Porter, referring to the then Bishop of Durham's controversial remarks about the Resurrection, turned to me on the panel and announced: 'Vicar, you've got forty seconds to tell us about the Resurrection.' I responded: 'I am not going to talk about this huge mysterious event in forty seconds.' After a pause in which Janet Street-Porter seemed at a loss for words, but seeing she could not budge me, she allowed

136

a longer conversation. Ken Livingstone, who was also on the panel, told me afterwards how much he had learned about Christianity from that discussion.

Rolling back the clouds of amnesia and remembering what has been given and entrusted to the Church, is not a trip down memory lane. Edwin Muir in *The Journey Back* puts it well: 'Seek the beginnings, learn from where you come and know the various earth of which you are made.'[10] It is a long process of reaching down to the haunting, elemental memories of oppression, deliverance, exodus, exile and return of the Jewish people, leading to the announcement of the Kingdom of God in the ministry of Jesus through to the Passion, Good Friday and Easter, and wherever in the life of the Church that radical calling to live out those memories 'by faith' has taken place.

Surrounding Biblical words with so much metaphysical glory makes us feel safe listening to them. But the words of the prophets in their critique of religion and politics only come down to us as heard by their contemporaries, and later to the disciples of Jesus with no other authority than that of their inherent persuasiveness. Their truths have to be embodied.

A friend from the USA accompanying me to Evensong at St Paul's Cathedral told me: 'The trouble with you Brits is that when you have problems with the text you set it to music.' He referred specifically to the *Magnificat* with those disturbing words: 'He hath put down the mighty from their seat; and hath exalted the humble and meek. He hath filled the hungry with good things and the rich he hath sent empty away.'

There are many witnesses to the faith I am describing.

In the early 1980s St James's hosted the Zamani Soweto Sisters, a group of women who emerged out of the trauma of the 1976 uprisings in Soweto when many young people were killed by South African police.[11] The women, some of them mothers of children who had been murdered, formed themselves into a collective which trained women in literacy, sewing and dress making. They became famous for their patchwork quilts and exhibited them in St James's. I invited the Soweto Sisters to preach on Sunday and to sing for us. These women became our teachers. They had managed to turn their lives around and showed us another world is possible. Above everything they displayed a hope and confidence in the future. Their songs: songs of freedom, protest and promise of deliverance and a better life, echoed the songs of defiance and deliverance in the Bible.

These promises celebrated in this way are destabilizing for those who manage the status quo. I had to ask the South African security officials, sent by the embassy, not to harass the women. The women were of course more than capable of looking after themselves.

The Zamani Sisters demonstrated that a prerequisite for experiencing the confidence in hope for a better world is first acknowledging and naming their grief and their rage. This means helping those who do not understand the despair of their situation to acknowledge it, and those who know what it is to be oppressed but cannot find the means to express their grief. Only then, once through that narrow gateway, will there be a home coming. Sometimes there is a lot of waiting! Patience is a revolutionary virtue, or, as Jesus put it: 'Blessed are you that weep now for you shall laugh.'

When the image of the exile begins to resonate then two aspects of the prophetic imagination can be identified.

The first shows that this imaginative activity does not reform or destroy tradition, but stays rigorously close to the text, to the world behind the text, the text itself and to the questions asked of the text. Staying close to the text means paying attention to the language. There has to be a reserve about public use of language itself, to the oddness of the strange world of the Bible. This means fostering a reticence in public about the use of Christian language. So much Christian talk is either misunderstood or not understood at all.

The second aspect shows that imaginative activity stays rigorously close to the experience of ambivalence, disturbance, grief expressed and apathy dispelled. As the psychiatrist RD Laing observed: 'We do not need theories so much as the experience – although the theory comes later.'

As those who experienced the Zamani Soweto Sisters proved, a new word could be uttered, new songs be sung and new actions be taken.

My unqualified welcome prevented the St James's community from turning into a cranky, dissenting and exclusive sect. 'What are we supposed to do?' people regularly asked me, sometimes with an aggressive tone from those who felt threatened, but more usually as a genuine query, expressing perplexity with difficult issues. It is not easy dismantling idols. 'Stick with the questions,' I answered, 'Talk about them, get together with others and see where it leads.'

Some people left, including most of the small congregation I inherited. One Christmas Eve during the sermon a dozen people sitting in the gallery walked out. They were staying at the Ritz Hotel nearby. A year later a Public Relations person from the hotel called me in some embarrassment to ask what I planned to preach. When I told her, no one from the hotel came to the Midnight Service; they went instead to St Paul's Cathedral to listen to the Bishop of London.

I did not proselytize. People have to make up their own minds. I resisted manipulating people as Billy Graham's evangelists tried to do to me in Cambridge. I had no wish to make people like me, in order to justify myself and so feel under no obligation to change my beliefs. However, I did whatever I could to be as persuasive as possible. People have to decide for themselves. That cannot be emphasized too much.

So Walter Brueggemann helped remove the road block. Meanwhile Episcopal and other eyebrows were raised concerning a number of activities at St James's.

Hello. You are very welcome. This is who we are and what we do. What would you like to do?
Hello, come in. You are very welcome. Thank you for accepting our invitation.
Hello, come in. You are very welcome. Is there anything we can do to help?

No questions asked about religious belief, political persuasion or sexual orientation. Everyone was welcome.

This unqualified and unconditional welcome became the springboard for all our activities. I said 'Yes' to every idea, every proposal, even while a more complex and often chaotic organization emerged. I insisted on not excluding anyone. There were no boundaries. The poor, the jobless and those without anywhere to live were welcome, gays, transsexuals, families, children, young and the elderly, artists and accountants as well as the prosperous. Labour supporters felt more comfortable there than the Tories. John Gummer, then Chairman of the Conservative Party, once phoned to complain that

I never invited Conservative speakers. I had just arranged a lecture series on 'Marxism and Christianity' which provided an opportunity for public debate usually confined to academia. I asked him for a list of Conservative speakers, but got no response, although Norman Tebbit among other right-wing politicians did take part in public discussions.

Projects were established. Some flourished, others withered, others moved to more spacious venues elsewhere in London.

In 1982 a Centre for Health and Healing was established. This hosted clinics, counselling, lectures and seminars on complementary medicine. Therapists and a doctor staffed a permanent clinic and once a week offered free treatment to people off the street. They sat on the rectory staircase and draped themselves round the banisters waiting for a consultation. After twelve years the director Beverly Martin, building on her experience in Piccadilly, established the Marian Association in North London. Today the association offers validated MA courses in psychotherapy and healing.

The year 1982 also saw the early stages of hospitality offered to New Age groups, about which more later. They remain a significant feature of St James's.

For eight years an annual Piccadilly Arts Festival took place.

In 1984 I commissioned Peter Dickinson to write a Mass for the Tercentenary Celebration.

The *Mass for the Apocalypse* was performed liturgically at that year's festival, given its title from the festival's theme, 'Festival of the Apocalypse', inspired by George Orwell's *1984*.

The theme attracted the celebrated Russian film director Andrei Tarkovsky, who accepted our invitation to give a lecture alongside a showing of his films, some at the British Academy of Film and Television Arts (BAFTA), a few doors down from the church on Piccadilly, the rest in the rectory sitting room.

This meant his travelling from the Soviet Union, and the festival hit the headlines when on arrival he decided to defect.

So many people turned up for his lecture at BAFTA, which could only host a limited number, that we transferred the event to the church, where he addressed a thousand silently attentive listeners for several hours on the spiritual condition of the Russian people and the rest of the world.

Sweltering in a very hot summer, people crammed into the rectory sitting room to watch Tarkovsky's films and we produced trays of iced fruit juices ready to revive the intrepid audiences when they staggered out. Most of the audiences were so moved by the beauty of Tarkovsky's films that they put up with the discomfort.

Tarkovsky became a friend. Knowing that I had been invited to visit the Soviet Union as part of a delegation arranged by the British Council of Churches he asked me to visit his family, who were suffering persecution as a result of his defection. He expressed particular concern about his young son, only eleven years old. Tarkovsky knew that if he returned to Moscow he would never be permitted to leave again, nor be given the freedom to make more films.

He had several ideas, including a film of *Hamlet*, in which he hoped to cast Roger Rees from the Royal Shakespeare Company, an actor he particularly admired and most wished to meet; and a life of St Anthony about which he spoke eloquently, vividly recreating the 'temptations' for us in cinematic terms at several of our meetings.

Before dying of cancer a few years later he managed to complete only two more films, *Nostalgia* in Italy and *Sacrifice* in Sweden, heartbreakingly autobiographical and hauntingly beautiful chamber pieces about his exile from not only Russia but also the West, a world he considered to be over-obsessed with materialism.

The idea surfaced that, since I was going to Moscow, I could bring his son back to Britain and then 'adopt' him so he could be closer to his father. I visited Tarkovsky's family in Moscow, and met young Andrei. However, KGB officials made it plain that the boy would not be allowed out of the Soviet Union – reminding us pointedly that his father could always return there: he had the choice.

While Tarkovsky was dying of cancer, the KGB relented. After his death, a right-wing Italian organization offered sanctuary to his wife and son, and I never saw them again.

The poet and artist William Blake also provided inspiration for the 1984 festival. Since he had been baptized at St James's in the winter of 1757, we inaugurated a William Blake Society in 1985. This organization continues to this day honouring and celebrating Blake the artist, engraver, poet, prophet and visionary.

George Goyder became the society's first president. He was a businessman and a devoted supporter of the Church of England, a pioneer in developing laypeople in its governance. Together with Kathleen Raine, Adrian Mitchell and many others, he put together ambitious programmes including a reading of Blake's complete work – a Blakethon. They commissioned Julia Usher, who had composed the *Mass of the Son Rising* at St Peter's Morden, to write A *Grain of Sand in Lambeth*, a setting for sixteen voices and small orchestra on texts from Blake's epic prophetic books.

The author Philip Pullman is now President of the Blake Society.

Three years later Matthew Fox, the Dominican monk who founded Creation Spirituality, visited London. His book *Original*

Blessing, intellectually rigorous as well as visionary, is pivotal in the understanding of this distinctive movement, which avoids the sentimental excesses of some New Age thinking. After his visit, St James's established a centre for Creation Spirituality. Matthew Fox became a friend and paid many subsequent visits to Britain, considering St James's his home. The centre formed a charity, Green Spirit, to build on and take further the work of Creation Spirituality.[12]

Theologians criticize Matthew Fox because he challenges traditional understandings of the Fall and Sin. He makes people think about creation and cosmology, and our place within it, drawing on the wisdom from different cultures over the ages, native wisdom going back millennia, and finds inspiration in Christian thinkers past and present, influential people who wrote at times of crisis in the Church, names like Meister Eckhart and formidable women such as Teresa of Avila and Hildegard von Bingen. Matthew Fox talks about creation and the universe: how our understanding of it in the light of scientific discovery should evoke awe and gratitude. Hence the title of his book: *Original Blessing*. At a time of universal concern about global warming and what we human beings are doing to our planet and to each other, his thinking has a contemporary resonance.

Matthew Fox took part in a number of public debates at St James's. He spoke about the wisdom of great thinkers from the past as though they were in the room with us. He explored the mystical tradition, the romantic poets, maverick theologians, artists and musicians whom we take for granted and know little about but whose work gains potency in the context of Creation Spirituality.

The New Age programme which I supported under the banner first of Turning Points then as Alternatives caused the most upset in the Church of England. Vicious attacks over many years are a reminder that differences in religion are no idle game.

My own interest in the New Age went back to 1968. During my stay in Chicago I wanted to discover the reasons for the extraordinary events in those days. Were they just an explosion of frustration against the war in Vietnam and a consequence of the upsurge of the Civil Rights Movement or was there more going on?

After failing to find any help from theologians I came across the scholar Theodore Roszak's *The Making of a Counter Culture*. Roszak was a history professor. For him the alienation of young people from their mostly affluent parents and all authority represented a revolt against what he calls 'technocracy': the technocratic, industrial military complex of the 1960s in the USA. Roszak explains that human life is diminished when creativity is sidelined. He quotes TS Eliot's *The Confidential Clerk*, where Sir Claude Mulhauser, a successful financier, dreams of being a famous potter. But the worlds of pottery and finance have to be kept separate. His talents as a successful businessman are judged on an altogether different level from his skills as a potter.

The question which *The Making of a Counter Culture* raises is not: How shall we organize, manage and fix reality? but: How shall we live? 'The primary aim of the counter culture is to proclaim a new heaven and a new earth . . . so marvellous, so wonderful, that the claims of technical expertise must of necessity withdraw to a subordinate and marginal status.'[13]

The argument continues: the age of technocracy *is* ending, or *will* end – the verbs are significant – to give way to a New Age, the Age of Aquarius, signalling the birth of a new world. As the musical *Hair* describes it:

Peace will guide the planets, and
Love will steer the stars.
Harmony and understanding,
Sympathy and trust abounding,
No more falsehoods or derision.
Golden living dream of visions,
Mystic revelation and mind's true liberation.

However, the New Age had not arrived in the 1980s.

Samuel Beckett put it succinctly: 'We are living at the end of an era in between death and a difficult birth.'

Shortly a new age will be forced on the planet because of the economic, political and social effects of global warming – rather different from the world of love, harmony and peace imagined by the Aquarians.

I was determined to discover what lay behind the often bizarre, sometimes barmy, frequently life-enhancing activities of the New Age. Did I miss something? What could I learn from them? And why did they upset some people so much?

In May 1989 a magazine called *Prophecy Today*, with a circulation of about fifty thousand, had on its front cover a photograph of St James's Piccadilly with the word 'Deception' slashed across it and the words: 'evil men and imposters will go from bad to worse deceiving and being deceived'. Under the editorial title 'Enter the Apostate Church', the editor wrote how he had already complained to the Bishop of London that I was teaching heresy and not preaching the pure Gospel based on Biblical authority (rather a different Bible to the one I was in the process of discovering).

I felt irritation and alarm: irritation because yet again I had to explain myself, and alarm because to accuse anyone of deception and apostasy is to settle a curse on their heads; and the penalty is death. The article represented a public attack that had been simmering ever since I arrived. Sadly we had to take measures to revise and increase security arrangements.

These attacks annoyed me because I always had an ambivalent attitude to New Age thinking. My offer of welcome to Alternatives did not signify whole-hearted agreement. The church was a public forum. But I expressed criticism of what seemed sentimental and superficial. Some New Age teachings were just wrong: illness is not cured by relief of toxins; cancer patients are not cured by recitation of daily affirmations. Some of the therapies advocated created a world of fantasy-like searching for the 'lost child' or the 'inner child', thus 'completing' our childhood. All reinforced a relentless and all-pervasive concern for 'me' and 'me alone'. Reality, they claimed, did not exist beyond the 'me'.

Alternatives invited me to speak regularly at their meetings. Once I was speaking the day before members of the St James's congregation planned a demonstration outside the Home Office in response to Michael Howard, then Home Secretary, bringing to Parliament a particularly poisonous piece of legislation on Immigration. I invited the audience of some two hundred to join the protest. Embarrassed, one of the team organizing Alternatives said to me: 'Donald, we are very aware' – meaning: we are thinking about you, but that's as far as we are going.

I criticized the 'pick-and-mix' approach to spirituality, choosing from the shelves whatever appealed at that particular moment, like sweets on a supermarket shelf.

Sometimes I saw people emerging from Alternatives looking lost, confused – easy prey for self-styled gurus. It reminded me of a disturbing occasion when I taught English in Beirut, trying to help those who were not at home in any language. A young man of around twenty came to me in despair. He spoke some Arabic, some English, some Turkish, some German, some Greek, and was incoherent in all of them. It is the same today for those who ransack the shelves in the pick-and-mix market of modern spirituality.

But there was much I appreciated about the New Age, for example the Gaia Hypothesis by James Lovelock, which declared that the earth should be regarded as a living organism with interrelated paths, showing that all living creatures are inextricably linked. This hypothesis has been a significant influence on not only New Age thinkers. I appreciated New Age teaching on mindfulness and meditation, which echoed parts of the Christian tradition, and I responded to the expressed needs for developing rituals around the passing on of wisdom, mourning loss and marking life-changes – ceremonies which then barely featured in the prayer book revisions of mainstream Anglican churches. I particularly admired the work of Elisabeth Kübler-Ross on healing, grief, terminal illness and death.

At its best Alternatives attracted those men and women working on the frontiers of the old culture and peering into a future world. The psychiatrists David Bohm and Fritjof Kapra, who spoke at St James's on the relationship between science and religion, were two such thinkers. Father Bede Griffiths, who while remaining rooted in the Catholic tradition, combined East and West in his person, and lived in the Shantivanam Ashram in India. Father Bede arrived in my study and after being greeted by Mackerel and Tyger, sat in silence with me for half an hour. Then he looked up, smiled and said: 'That was a good meeting!'

It was clear that many people coming to Alternatives were disenchanted by mainline Churches. Bored by meaningless repetitive worship and the lack of interest in spiritual matters by many clergy, they felt drawn to the New Age to explore alternatives. I made a point of welcoming them to St James's, talking to them individually and in groups saying: 'We are sorry about your experience of Christianity. Please tell us your story. One day you might like to listen to ours.' There were many conversations.

On Christmas Eve 1980 twelve people gathered at the rectory, responding to an advertisement: 'If you are alone on Christmas Eve, come to St James's Piccadilly for a party.'

Sitting in the large empty rectory over Christmas while homeless people shivered outside on Piccadilly, I felt the need to do something. I had no idea who would come. Some members of the congregation had provided a French-style buffet with freshly baked baguettes, cheeses from Harrods, home-made Cordon Bleu pâtés, cooked vegetable salads and mince pies.

Mark, Ernie, Jim and George who made St James's their patch turned up with their friends and sat together talking quietly, comparing notes on the meagre Christmas social services being provided by the Westminster City Council. They at first sat on the landing of the rectory then moved into the sitting room.

Hilda dominated the proceedings. She became a prominent figure in the church in the early days, turning up to all events, carrying her personal belongings in four plastic bags. A tall, slim, upright woman in her late fifties, she wore a hat at all times, the sort my mother wore during the war years. Her educated tone and manner went together with an often overpowering smell of stale urine.

Hilda came up to me and sniffed: 'The food's not up to much!'

After the buffet some members from the Covent Garden Chorus arrived, having offered to provide entertainment on their evening off, and stood on the staircase above the main landing where the tramps, looking ill at ease, were still picking at cheese and pâté. In loud operatic voices the chorus sang carols and songs from the shows to the uncomfortable audience. The tramps gradually disappeared into side rooms, rolling their eyes.

I saw they were settling in for the night, so I invited them to the Midnight Mass, and they quickly left, taking the rest of the food with them.

Some months later Hilda, who slept regularly in one of the shop doorways on Jermyn Street, disappeared. She had told a member of the congregation about wanting to visit France. Perhaps she had moved there. We never saw her again.

That Christmas Eve reminded me of Buñuel's film *Viridiana*, where society outcasts are invited into a mansion by a nun who out of the Christian kindness of her heart wants to do good. In the film they take the place over. The house is trashed and she ends up raped. The Piccadilly friends were better behaved unlike Buñuel's underclass in a film that excoriates both society's heartlessness and hypocrisy in its treatment of those it wants to ignore: the disabled and mentally sick.

The rectory was no longer just a private home, but the centre from which many projects and activities spread. Within six years ten makeshift offices had been fashioned out of sculleries, junk rooms and corridors. All criteria for health and safety would have failed.

Slowly, as I hoped, a congregation emerged.

At the beginning I peered round the vestry door to see if anyone had come for the Sunday Eucharist. Then as numbers improved I stood in the entrance porch and welcomed people as they arrived in ones and twos. Sometimes I went out to Piccadilly, surprising unsuspecting tourists and bringing them into the church.

After five years the congregation amounted to around five hundred, coming from all over London and even beyond, on a weekly, monthly or quarterly basis. All considered St James's their church. I had no wish to build up a narrow, enclosed, intolerant church advocated by *Prophecy Today*. St James's was a ragged and open community.

Committees can be the death of voluntary organizations. To avoid the committee disease I 'sounded a call'. That quaint phrase describes a particular invitation responding to whatever need I or others identified at a particular time. 'If you are not serious about this idea or prepared to be serious about it, don't bother,' I would tell everyone who came. The positive response exceeded what I anticipated.

All kinds of groups emerged. One became a campaign on behalf of and together with the jobless and young homeless in London. Others passionate about injustice and poverty recalled the actions of an angry Jesus and the words of Isaiah: 'Shame on you, you who make unjust laws, and publish burdensome decrees, depriving the poor of justice, robbing the weakest of my people of their rights, despoiling the widow and plundering the orphan.' (Isaiah 10, verses 1-2) These groups were as fiery and committed as those in evangelical churches who revelled in quoting Biblical texts damning homosexuals.

I commissioned a study to find out what went on in Central London at night. Inspired by the work of Franciscans in San Francisco

I wanted to see if there was anything we could do; perhaps establish an all-night-café on Piccadilly. For five months the researcher Simon Cregeen began to build up a picture of who was on the streets in Central London at night, finding out what they needed or wanted and seeing what provision already existed for them. London churches eventually used this well-researched project for educational purposes, and St Martin-in-the-Fields established a café as part of its London Connection programme.

In January 1987 the weather suddenly deteriorated; forecasters warned the Thames could be frozen. Returning late from visiting friends in Bethnal Green I began to walk back to the West End, noticing doorways crammed with people, mostly teenagers, huddled together to keep warm. The next morning I recited Morning Prayer in a warm and empty church. 'This is ridiculous,' I said to myself. 'We will open the church for anyone to come and sleep here while the cold weather lasts.'

Together with a couple from the congregation we called the West End agencies and churches concerned with homelessness but all the phones were engaged. We decided to go ahead on our own, despite being aware that what we did would be criticized as a stunt.

We announced a press conference so the media could meet with those we called 'our guests'. But since 'our guests' are not the kind of people who get to see press releases no one showed up except a journalist and a butler from the Ritz Hotel bringing trays of profiteroles.

We hired a van and drove to where we knew people gathered and invited them. News spread. For five nights we provided accommodation in the church for more than two hundred a night, mostly young people. The Women's Royal Voluntary Service provided soup, breakfast and blankets. Nothing was too much trouble for these indomitable women in their thick green tweed suits and berets.

The media took an interest and forced politicians to take action. Edwina Currie, a junior Health Minister, turned up disguised in a headscarf to investigate. She had earlier issued a statement that old people who could not afford winter heating should knit themselves woolly hats and jumpers.

As I had anticipated I received considerable criticism from organizations who considered it their job to take care of the young homeless. Correctly they pointed out that our amateurish and often chaotic action gave the impression that this kind of response constituted an appropriate method of dealing with this type of crisis, rather than a strategic initiative from the public sector. I agreed with their criticism and in interviews made this point repeatedly. But whenever I became 'political' the interview terminated.

As the weather improved the guests departed and the project scaled down.

Fourteen years later as I hailed a cab the driver looked at me and said: 'I remember you. Weren't you the vicar at that church in Piccadilly who opened the doors during the Big Freeze? Have this one on me, guv!'

The rectory was a busy centre; everyone was motivated, prepared to work hard and for long hours. We managed to sustain this level of creativity for many years. I took easily to being an entrepreneur, since other people's success made me happy; but being a manager was a different matter, finding it difficult to deal with interpersonal differences and inevitable disagreements focusing mostly on limited space and budget. What I learned years later in the Balkans would have helped me at Piccadilly. Mediating between perpetrators of crimes and survivors was straightforward compared to dealing with church council meetings!

Management consultants were called in to look at the way we tried to work together. They came and went; diagrams were drawn with arrows pointing in many directions. But they told us nothing new.

Peter Pelz lived in the rectory with me for the first seven years, while working as coordinator of the Arts Festivals. Mackerel and Tyger were always ready to welcome any newcomer. Guests came regularly to stay from all over the world.

Then in 1983 Archbishop Trevor Huddleston, famous for his book *Naught for Your Comfort*, which alerted the world to the evils of apartheid, and friend to Nelson Mandela and Archbishop Tutu, came to live in the rectory. After his controversial ministry in South Africa, Trevor Huddleston returned to Britain and became a no-less-fiercely political Bishop of Stepney before being invited to Mauritius as Archbishop of the Indian Ocean. When he retired he needed a London base to continue his struggle to end apartheid in his new role as President of the Anti-Apartheid Movement.

Shy and reticent personally the archbishop lived in the rectory for nine years. He kept himself private, enjoying his own company as a balance to his prominently public and campaigning life. He often told me about wanting to end his days in Piccadilly, because he knew people working there would keep an eye on him without intruding. When I was thinking it was time I move on he tried to get me on the shortlist for the Anglican Representative at the United Nations – unsuccessfully.

Through the archbishop I met and had many conversations with African leaders, particularly those who had served time on Robben Island. When visiting London they always called at the rectory to meet Bishop Trevor and thank him for his struggle and witness on their behalf. Nelson Mandela told me: 'No white person has done more for South Africa than Trevor Huddleston.' At our meeting Nelson Mandela gave me all his attention as though I were the most important person in the world, as he thanked me for providing a home for Trevor.

The person who introduced me to Bishop Trevor became one of the most important people in my life during my time at Piccadilly and beyond.

In 1979 Nadir Dinshaw, a Pakistani businessman, known for his philanthropic work and generous support of unpopular causes, happened to be watching a BBC broadcast of a Harvest Festival from St Peter's Morden. He heard me start my sermon on the consequences of the destruction of the earth's ecology. At the end of the service I pointedly withheld the Blessing, because of the mess we were making of the planet. Intrigued by this gesture, Nadir asked our mutual friend, Jim Thompson, then Bishop of Stepney, to arrange a meeting.

There began a friendship which lasted over twenty-two years until his death in 2002.

He and his family supported me generously, and continue to do so. Nadir had a special gift for friendship and an extraordinary capacity for stepping into another person's shoes. Like the Chinese sage who did not need 'to step out of his front door to travel the world, nor gaze out of this window to know the path of the stars', Nadir, always reassuring, encouraging, constructively critical and attentive, saw his vocation as offering friendship to me and to countless others. At times of crisis in my work Nadir, who could recite from memory a vast treasury of poetry and prose, would quote George Eliot's words: 'When death, the great reconciler has come, it is never our tenderness that we repent of – only our severity.'

However, Nadir himself could be severe when necessary: passionately so in the cause of justice, and particularly against government policies which discriminated against anyone on grounds of poverty, race, refugee status, religion, gender or sexual orientation. At St James's we witnessed this passion in the sermons he preached. He told me that these invitations to speak in public encouraged him to do more. He was a fine writer, his mellifluous style and quiet manner of speaking, naming and shaming politicians and public figures, made his sermons memorable. I learned from his preaching not to be embarrassed by the concreteness of his language.

For the next twenty-two years he provided an anchor for me. Though mystified by my support of the New Age, he nonetheless appreciated the breadth of my welcome. Whenever I shared some outlandish idea with him he would shake his head, look at me with his large, sad dark eyes and say: 'Dearest Donald . . .'

Nadir died in December 2002. I happened to be in Bosnia being driven late at night from Banja Luka to Sarajevo in a blizzard. We lost our way and the car nearly overturned on one of the tricky bends through the mountains of central Bosnia. During this perilous drive I received a message on my mobile that Nadir had suffered a massive heart attack and was dying. My inner landscape crumbled. His death has been an irreparable loss.

In 1992 I moved out of the rectory. One evening while having a bath, I heard a knock on the bathroom door. Before I could answer, an elderly man poked his head round the door saying: 'Sorry, I am looking for the Dunamis meeting.'

St James's rented a flat for me first in Piccadilly, then for a while near Baker Street (from where for a few months I motorcycled to work, until one day I fell off the bike and it crashed into a lamp-post). Peter Pelz, who had become a full-time artist, moved permanently to a house we shared near Oxford to paint commissions and prepare work for exhibitions. I then moved into the recently retired verger's flat next to the church.

As required by law I informed the Diocese of London of my movements and activities, and paid regular visits to the bishop, as I have already described, to be gently or not so gently reprimanded. I was surprised that after ten years at St James's no one asked me how I was getting on. When I discussed the matter of shortage of office space and the need to live elsewhere, diocesan officials told me firmly: 'You have a rectory; live in it.'

One reason for leaving the rabbit warren of the rectory was to free up more space, another to create a less frenetic atmosphere and make the rectory more welcoming – particularly to the many people who wanted to see me for counselling and other matters.

The days of the religious redcoat were over; now all kinds of people with every sort of problem wanted a piece of my time.

The number of people who asked to see me caught me unawares. Given my resolve to offer an unqualified welcome this should not have been surprising. The Centre for Health and Healing, the caravan, an able team of assistant priests and several wise women from the congregation were kept busy listening, encouraging, offering advice, guiding people to the relevant agencies and being available.

I had no formal training as a counsellor or therapist but an opportunity for reflecting on my own life became a bonus.

Fourteen years before my arrival in Piccadilly, just after being ordained, I wrote to the psychiatrist Anthony Storr, whom I had heard on the radio, asking to see him. I came from a family where personal matters were never discussed. I was nervous. As Ian McEwan in *On Chesil Beach* writes, describing the early days of courtship between Edward and Florence: 'The language and practice of therapy, the currency of feelings diligently shared, mutually analyzed, were not in general circulation. While one heard of wealthier people going in for psychoanalysis it was not yet customary to regard oneself in everyday terms, as an enigma, as an exercise in narrative history, or a problem waiting to be solved.'[14] I could not believe that anyone would be interested in my story, even if they were being paid to listen.

I kept my meeting with Antony Storr secret. People told me of his sympathetic ear and understanding but he was not interested. It was an unpromising meeting. I wish I had never gone. He had a list of questions and recorded each answer with a tick or a cross. 'Do you notice men or women in the street?' came the first question. 'Both,' I replied. The questions went on from there. Finally he announced: 'I can't take you on. But I will refer you to the Open Way Clinic.'

There I met VV Alexander, who became my therapist for five years. Slowly I began to trust him. Nothing appeared to shock him. He was always there, attentive, mostly motionless and holding my gaze. Occasionally, when he felt tired, he would say 'Excuse me' and stand on his head for several minutes.

Bored with my stories and dreams I sometimes embroidered them just to please him. He fastened on to one recurring dream which we analysed fruitlessly again and again. I am walking on a beach. The sea is on my right. In the distance there are two teenagers, a boy and a girl holding hands. I try to reach them. Obstacles appear. I cannot move, stuck, bogged down in the sand. I invented a word for this: stogged. I never reached the young couple. Then he proposed I undertake a supervised course of LSD. I was just starting my work at Morden; I was scared as to what might happen, so I declined.

The therapy ended with several sessions of psychodrama which took place above a shoe shop in Queens Road, off the Bayswater Road in London. Eight men, all with bushy beards except for myself, met under the guidance of Jerome Liss, one of the directors of the New Age Center Big Sur on the edge of the Pacific between Los Angeles and San Francisco. He invited us to tell our stories. When it came to my turn I first had to play myself as a baby. In spite of the beards I enjoyed being held while gurgling away. Then Jerome Liss told me to play my mother. I started. Then I broke down. Suddenly I understood her situation and her life, the reasons for her behaviour. She did her best. I could forgive her. Even though I had already done this, years earlier, the long process of therapy culminating in the psychodrama helped complete the process.

Having been listened to, I could now do the same to others. I gained insight into my own behaviour and motivation. This enabled me to become a better listener. That is what I had learnt, but still I had to live on my wits.

One evening at a church meeting I noticed a man in his thirties, fastidiously dressed, who asked to see me. He followed me around as I locked the church and followed me to my study. Alone in the rectory I doubted the wisdom of my invitation. Clerical collars can attract psychotic and deranged people.

As I feared he became agitated and angry. Having told me about his work as teacher at a London Art College, his painting and girl-friend, he then began to pace the room, eyes narrowing. Expecting him to attack me at any moment I got up and told him firmly to stand still. Then I went over to him, put my arms round him, held him very tight and said: 'God loves you. I love you,' again and again. Then when he had calmed down I asked him: 'What do you see when you look at me?' What I was trying to do was to draw him out of his mad state. I forced him to look at the pictures, the books, the flowers, the icons. When he had recovered I told him to see a doctor.

We met twice after that and he invited me to his studio to show me his paintings. Worried about not being able to help him I urged him to have treatment. I sensed his madness returning. The story has a happy ending. The last time I saw him happened months later. He turned up with a black South African woman. They were going to be married and live in New York. He had come to thank me.

Ignorant of the guidelines proposed for therapists I had broken many cardinal rules. For example, the therapist does not hold some-one in their arms and tell that person: 'I love you.'

My subsequent encounters were less dramatic and I took care to meet people in a safe environment.

A steady procession of people arrived at the rectory wanting to know about Christianity. Mostly these constituted serious enquir-ies, dissatisfied atheists, disillusioned agnostics, refugees from the New Age, all looking for a Christianity and a Church not stuck in the mindset of a Victorian Sunday School. There were those who responded to the writings and sermons by the then Bishop of Dur-ham, David Jenkins. In four years he had received ten thousand let-ters. He and I talked of establishing an informal network, but it did not materialize. Then Margaret Thatcher responded to one of his statements. She described the bishop as a cuckoo. So we launched the Cuckoo Club. For a small donation club members received a badge; two thousand pounds was collected and went to a youth project in Leeds.

The sheer mass of these enquiries led to problems. Many joined the church looking for friendship, wanting to fit in. 'Getting to know you' became a preoccupation for the community at St James's. Apart from a natural desire to welcome new people, this preoccupation was a reflection of the fashion beyond the church for developing closeness with others, a search for intimacy. To meet these needs churches form small groups. Then disagreements, rivalries and jealousies occur and much time is spent on trying to sort them out. Not everyone wants to belong to a group when most of their working lives are dominated by meetings and team activity. These people fit in with difficulty.

There were also problematic meetings with people considering ordination from St James's, but also from other churches.

A man in his thirties, working in the City, wanted to be ordained. He told me about his partner, who had been married. After living together for three years they could not decide whether to marry. He had had other relationships. He wanted to know what he should tell the bishop about his relationships. We talked through this problem at great length. He decided to keep quiet about his private life, but if he was asked, as he was, then he would say he had a girlfriend, whom he saw from time to time.

He belonged to a generation which did not consider that he 'lived in sin' and should 'repent'. So he lied. He is now ordained, married and a vicar.

It is wrong that at a crucial, life-changing time, a person has to lie.

Some are not prepared to do so. Another man wanted to be ordained. His bishop told him that his future as a priest depended on his being celibate. This person had a male partner. He could not give the bishop an assurance that he would be celibate. So he was told he could not be ordained. The congregation from which he came were nonplussed, then angry. However, had he lied he would have been ordained.

The Church of England makes pronouncements about justice but cannot see the injustice within its own gates.

There is a cartoon: a beaming vicar stands outside the church door as two gay men approach. He smiles at them and says: 'Thank you for not coming.'

One day a woman from Harlow in Essex came to see me. Married with three children and a husband who worked in London, she attended yoga classes while the children were at school. The high point of her week became a woman's yoga group. It helped her relax. She also enjoyed the socializing with the group: coffee mornings and lunches were the high point of her social life. She had been persuaded to join an Alpha Course introducing her to a stringently evangelical form of Christianity. In the group she told everyone about her enjoyment of yoga. The group leader asked to see her afterwards and told her that yoga 'is of the Devil' and she must decide to give up either yoga or membership of the church. She came to me in distress. After our meeting she decided to continue yoga and forget about the church.

Not all evangelicals and leaders of the Alpha Course behave so callously. Evangelicals are deeply divided. However, the conversation with that woman became only one in a stream of people wanting to see me with similar problems.

My advice stayed the same: never get into discussion with the kind of evangelical leader who has 'discovered the truth' and is 'born again'.

Eventually I set up Fundamentalist Anonymous to help ease people away from what had become an addictive and destructive type of religion.

Events overtook me, however.

In January 1995 I received an offer for a job from Thursdays, a group of former evangelicals, mostly young people, not all of them Church of England. I had met them over a period of months and they invited me to be their priest. They questioned me at length about my understanding of the Incarnation, Salvation and Redemption.

They used to meet for worship in rooms above a pub in Central London, not by choice. Searching for a redundant church they found nothing because most clergy were suspicious of them.

At first I thought they were a small splinter group but I soon realized they formed only part of a growing but disorganized network which while honouring their evangelical roots were genuinely serious, eager to discover Christianity in all its diversity and richness. Some of the leading members had come from All Souls Langham Place, a bastion of Church of England evangelicalism, others from Ichthus, a house church movement in South London.

They made a professional presentation of their aims: planning to establish a chapel for contemplation using modern multimedia technology to create an accessible space where people could 'take time out to be silent' – a centre for social action which would support and encourage this work; a centre for community arts providing opportunities for people to explore and express their creativity; and a centre for corporate worship, making use of modern communication facilities (sound systems, video projections, etc.) also drawing on the best of traditional liturgy. A group of thirty highly motivated professional people were all ready to take the project forward. Much detailed planning had taken place. All they wanted was a vicar who together with other clergy would be their leader and provide a link with the Church of England.

This was an extraordinary invitation from an evangelical group to a radical liberal priest. The group could offer no accommodation or money. I accepted on condition they found a church and told them I would have to continue as Rector of St James's for the time being. I was thrilled to be associated with such a risky venture.

However, circumstances changed. In August 1995 after months of increasing pain I began to feel seriously unwell. By September I had been diagnosed with cancer of the colon and admitted just in time to St Mark's Hospital Northwick Park for an operation.

My plans for Thursdays and everything else in my life had to be put on hold.

I took my prayer book, Bible and icons, put them on the locker next to my bed, but could not begin to say prayers or read the Bible. I felt too scared. Having written to my friends at St James's explaining my sudden disappearance, and asking for their prayers, I said to myself: 'They can do it for me,' and immediately felt better.

I made a good recovery quickly and returned to work on the Sunday before Christmas 1995. As the procession entered from the back of the church I noticed a large banner stuck on the reredos behind the altar: 'Welcome back, Donald'. I knew then in that moment that after fifteen years I had done what I could at St James's.

But what should I do next?

In the next two and a half years before I eventually left Piccadilly I spent much time considering and testing out new possibilities. This led to the founding of the Soul of Europe and to work in Bosnia.

Transition

After ten years at Piccadilly in 1990, five years before my operation, I had already begun to look for possibilities of other jobs in the Church of England. At fifty-six one more position might be available to me. I discussed this with Graham Leonard, the Bishop of London, before he retired. 'I won't stand in your way,' he said. This is bishop-speak for: 'You're on your own, sunshine.'

I quickly found this to be the case. No door opened for me anywhere.

On a pilgrimage to Mount Athos which I made with Robert Runcie, after his retirement, and James Thomson, Master of Charterhouse, Robert told me with a sigh: 'Had I been brave enough I would have seen you were a bishop.' Richard Holloway, then Bishop of Edinburgh, put it more bluntly: 'You were known as the Red Parson of Piccadilly supporting the New Age. Who in their right mind would make you a bishop or a dean?' He then added: 'And anyhow, is that what you really want?'

Returning to the church after my spell in hospital I could have carried on at St James's until I turned seventy, but I decided to leave before retirement. Many of the activities I started and encouraged had 'flown the nest'. Dunamis had come to an end after fifteen years, winding down after the fall of the Berlin Wall and the end of the Cold War. The Lufthansa Festival had moved to St John's Smith Square. The Café Project flourished at the London Connection based in St Martin-in-the-Fields. Alternatives and the Association for

Creation Spirituality had become charities. The Blake Society prospered, meeting at different London venues. The Centre for Health and Healing moved to North London.

St James's ran three businesses: the Wren Restaurant established in the former Parish Hall adjoining the church building on Jermyn Street, the Market trading in the courtyard five days a week, and a professional music programme. We had been advised to establish a trading company run by a chief executive and directors, of which I would be one. The chief executive's brief was to ensure 'maximization of profits'.

Making money now emerged as the number one priority. Held responsible for the church's 'spiritual' needs only, I felt sidelined, hemmed in, and found myself saying for the first time in fifteen years: 'As rector I have to remind you that I have the freehold, etc.' After my operation I found the many business meetings enervating. We were given bad advice and told to disband the company. The chief executive left and the Parochial Church Council eventually took responsibility.

This turn of events should have been anticipated. I was an example of what Max Weber, the sociologist, called the 'bureaucratization of charisma': a pioneer and initiator is taken over by the institution which emerges as a result of that leadership. The institution contradicts the original vision because in order to survive its priority is ensuring continuity and stability at any price.

I undertook some career counselling and began to explore a portfolio of different activities. I had seen too many clergy contemplating retirement, saying: 'I won't do anything for six months; then I'll see what's what.' By which time it is too late; all the networks will have fallen away.

By chance I developed a role as consultant for a multinational company in community affairs and business ethics. In 1984 I had established the St James's Business Houses Council, bringing local businesses together to support the church. Rio Tinto, then known as Rio Tinto Zinc, had its headquarters in the parish at No 6 St James's Square. The company had substantial shares in around fifty operations throughout the world, mining large high-quality mineral deposits. Its metal products include aluminium, copper, gold, and iron ore. It also produces coal, uranium, borax, diamonds and zinc. Rio Tinto became active members of the Business Houses Council, supporting our arts programme, sponsoring a sculpture garden, concerts by young musicians and banners for the church. As these contacts developed I began to receive abusive letters from Minewatch, a vociferous group attacking Rio Tinto's treatment of the environment. Minewatch accused me of being set up by Rio Tinto: a prominent liberal London cleric was being manipulated as part of the company's strategy to improve its image.

But I had already formed a working relationship with Platform, a group concerned with the impact of big business on the environment so I went to work for Rio Tinto with my eyes open.

The senior management at No 6 St James's Square then invited me to visit two of Rio Tinto's operations: Richards Bay Minerals in South Africa and the Rossing Mine in Namibia.

Rio Tinto had created three criteria for establishing stable conditions in which a mine should flourish: mutual respect, active partnership and long-term commitment. My brief was to determine how well these big ideas were being worked out in practice.

In a steep learning curve I carried out a full programme of meetings with individuals and organizations covering the spectrum of those particularly concerned with business in the community, from government ministers, union officials and mine managers to non-governmental organizations.

I accept the importance of mining in our modern world, and do not share Mark Twain's opinion that 'every man-made hole is a blasphemy'. But my first sight of the uranium mine at Rossing as I flew over Namibia was shocking. The slit in the desert, two miles long, half a mile deep, half a mile wide looked like a rape of the earth.

But what an astonishing feat of technology: power, transport systems, including a railway line to ferry the uranium to the coast, and the mine itself, crushing tons of rocks to find tiny scraps of uranium, essential to producing nuclear power; the crushing, sifting, refining, the maintaining of gigantic machines, and building dams to collect a steady supply of water for dampening the dust. Each day a thousand workers are bussed from a town thirty-five miles away.

What I witnessed reminded me of the awe-inspiring scene in Wagner's opera *Das Rheingold*, the start of his opera cycle, *Der Ring des Nibelungen*, when the gods descend into Nibelheim, home of the mining dwarves, who are now bound as slaves to hammer metal perpetually. Their tyrant master, Alberich, having foresworn human love and wrenched the gold from its home deep in the river, holds his hand up to show the ring fashioned from this earthly treasure: a ring which gives him power over the whole world and which the gods in turn want to steal from him. The slave masses shriek in subservience, cowering before his global might.

I saw myself as a mirror reflecting back everything people told me, pursuing difficult questions, encouraging and suggesting alternative approaches. Sometimes I had to be a counsellor. A stranger can often provide an opportunity for people to unburden themselves.

After a few days the words from St Matthew's Gospel came to me: 'Behold I send you forth as sheep in the midst of wolves; be ye therefore wise as serpents and harmless as doves.' (Matthew 10, verse 16)

The bottom line and priority for all multinational businesses are shareholders' interests, financial performance and operational excellence. Any philanthropic activity is regarded as enlightened self-interest. But new questions were and are being insistently and publicly raised about accountability to employers, to governments, countries and communities where mines function, and also to the environment. As the vice-president of Rio Tinto told me: 'We used to think community affairs was soft stuff; now it's the hardest.'

Andrew Hope, the managing director of Rossing, said: 'You legitimized conversation on difficult and troubling matters', and wrote later about my report on the visit: 'I found your visit and the report beneficial, particularly in helping us look at familiar issues from a fresh perspective.'

Following that letter and my participation in several activities at No 6 St James's Square under the umbrella of 'community affairs', Rio Tinto offered me a consultancy for one year from March 1998. This was the first building block for the portfolio.

A theological reflection on 'land' provided the postscript to my visit to South Africa. I recalled Albert Schweitzer's comment that no amount of reparation can repair the damage that white men have done to the African people. In Biblical language our connectedness with the land is reflected in a play on Hebrew words: Adam, humankind, and Adamah, earth, both linked in a covenantal relationship. In the Old Testament land is assigned to the whole community as a gift from God. This understanding of land clashed with the idea that land is regarded as a commodity, a gift. The Torah and the prophets understand the notion of land as inheritance in the face of the imperial system of apportioning land, practised by the pharaohs and by King Solomon. Ancient Israel's fundamental concern about land is that the weak have to be protected against the strong, which is the meaning of the tenth commandment: 'you shall not covet'. Every fifty years all debts are cancelled and the land is restored: this is the Jubilee – an inspiring picture of the Bible's promise of the kingdom of God where everyone and everything will flourish.

A number of regular church goers whom I met in South Africa and Namibia received my theological reflection which ended with the questions: 'How far is this critique valid for today? If it is true, what does it say about the mining industry?' 'How should decommissioning take place and the land be returned to the people?' 'Who owns the mine – just the shareholders in distant places? Or does the mine belong to the people? What people?'[15]

The critique received no response. Perhaps the questions are too difficult and uncomfortable.

Another building block for a portfolio emerged directly out of my work at Piccadilly. Clergy from Europe, the USA and Australia came regularly to investigate what we were doing; Germany, Switzerland and Scandinavia were especially interested. We organized 'zoo days'.

The Swedish clergy told me they felt more at home with us than with conservative evangelicals or Anglo-Catholics and our visibly active support for women priests and bishops constituted an added draw. As one Swedish priest told me: 'When my people want to know where I have been, I say to them: to London, to St James's.'

They invited me twice to Sweden. On the first visit in 1994 the Diocese of Lund asked me to meet the clergy, theologians and congregations to talk about opportunities for the Church there. Over fourteen years around two hundred Swedish clergy and ordinands had been to Piccadilly. A substantial programme gave time to explore these opportunities in more detail, share my experience and help clergy and laity reflect on their work. As a respected outsider, I was invited to contribute to an important debate about the weakening connection between the established Lutheran Church and the State.

Bishop Hammer, who later became Archbishop of Uppsala and the Chief Pastor of the Swedish Church, oversaw this shift in the relationship between Church and State. After meeting with the bishop I noticed, on leaving, a photograph of an ordination in which a bishop wore Episcopal ring, pectoral cross and carried a crozier, but no mitre. 'Do Swedish bishops not wear mitres?' I asked. 'Yes,' he replied, 'but the daughter of my predecessor took her father's mitre and turned it into a tea cosy.'

During a five-hour Bible study with a hundred ordinands we discussed the collapse of Enlightenment thinking and how to move on to new ways of reading ancient texts. One student came up to me in an interval and said: 'You really love the Bible, don't you!'

In September 1996 a group of clergy in Stockholm invited me to lead a conference on Christianity and the future of religion. The conference turned into a mission and a 'happening'. It took place in Stockholm Cathedral, which gave the event a public dimension no one had anticipated.

Public lectures on each of three evenings were followed by seminars the following days. Hundreds attended. Members of the Swedish government and leading Stockholm laity took part.

The theme of my addresses was exile and homecoming.

The cathedral stands next to the Old City, a medieval building untouched by the Reformation, with Renaissance and Baroque additions. I had asked the event organizers to create an environment which reflected the theme of the addresses. Each night a solemn procession carried a spectacular globe, lit from inside, to the main platform. Apples, oranges and lighted candles filled the side aisles; sprays of rosemary and thyme were placed in the pews. The congregation was invited to walk round the cathedral to look at specially commissioned paintings and outside in the cathedral garden wind chimes sounded among the trees.

Surprised by the welcome and trust from those who had invited me I threw away my text for twelve prepared talks. One priest told me afterwards: 'You did not speak *at* us, but *to* us and *with* us.'

This experience led me to want to establish a network for European city-centre churches and cathedrals. This became the second building block in my portfolio.

'The best is yet to come,' Robert Runcie, former Archbishop of Canterbury, wrote to me when I told him about my plans.

These carefully laid plans did not work out. After twelve months the consultancy at Rio Tinto ceased and those who knew me and might have renewed my contract had either left or retired. Those remaining looked for their own consultants. My proposals for future work with the Church in Sweden were enthusiastically received but lack of funds stopped further development. 'We will bear you in mind,' I was told.

Meanwhile my father's death in 1985 had altered my circumstances. It meant I could sell the family house in Chichester. While continuing my work at St James's I pooled my resources with Peter

Pelz, who had lived and worked with me on many projects throughout my time at Morden and in Piccadilly, and we bought a house together in the Cotswolds, where he spent the next ten years painting then running a coffeehouse.

I got to know my father better in his final years. We were different characters. He preferred to stay at home all day and do nothing. He sat in an old suit, or a dressing gown, sipping whisky, smoking his pipe and stroking Blackie, the long-haired cat, gazing out of the window at the unkempt garden. What did he think about? Someone came to just mow the lawn, but trees and shrubs which my mother, a keen gardener, had pruned so fastidiously now grew into a forest. The leylandii cypress trees which had served as a boundary with the neighbours were now so tall that in strong winter winds they shook alarmingly and could have crashed into the house. He seemed a little in awe of me. He said nothing apart from a greeting and a chuckle about bad weather and the leylandii, which eventually he allowed someone to prune, but I could see from the warmth and sparkle in his eyes that he loved me. His final years turned out to be the happiest for him. When it became clear he could not look after himself, and he did not want to move to London and live in the rectory with me, he went to live in a residential home near Liphook. My feelings of guilt turned out to be misplaced. Still a good-looking man in his eighties with a full shock of white hair, and the only male among the thirty residents there, the women spoiled and made a fuss of him. One day a few months before his death, I arrived to find him sitting close to an attractive graceful woman his own age. He introduced her as 'my girl'. Both suffered from memory loss. 'This,' he said, 'is Mrs What's-her-name.' To which she responded: 'And this is Mr What's-his-name.'

Plans for a portfolio had begun to unravel. I had vague notions of what I wanted to do, but no clarity. With no funding prospects, approaching retirement and having no position in the Church of England I tried to find an ecclesiastical perch, but this failed to materialize.

The millennium approached and I set about creating the European City Centre Churches Network. This was a mistake. I had intended to draw on my Piccadilly experience, but, aware that my work would soon be forgotten, I realized that a Central London Church of England parish would have little interest for churches in Helsinki, Budapest or Madrid. Temperamentally it is not in my nature to look back; I wanted to find something new and different.

Jeremy Paxman, who had been a guest speaker at one of St James's Business Houses lunches, and John Studzinski, then Vice-President at Morgan Stanley, told me that anything with 'church' in the title had no future. So the mouthful of European City Centre Churches Network turned eventually into the Soul of Europe.

Peter Pelz agreed to help and sold the coffeehouse. We pooled resources again, moved to a larger house with office space in Devon and from there set up the Soul of Europe.

Emma Nicholson, former Conservative and then Liberal Democrat MP of North Devon who got to know me during the dying of her husband, Michael Caine, encouraged us in this move: 'Devon is not as far as you think,' she said, and generously allowed us to lodge in her home while we searched for a house. Given the internet, it does not matter where a project headquarters are sited. 'You could run the Soul of Europe on a computer from a swamp in New Guinea,' she declared.

On 17th January 1999, some six months after leaving Piccadilly, the way forward became clear. That date marked the birth of the Soul of Europe.

Alan Jones, Dean of Grace Cathedral, San Francisco, had invited me to preach. Before that engagement thirty evangelical pastors who were 'church planting' asked me to lead a conference at St Juan Capistrano in California, helping them reflect on their work, their feelings about it and how they could do things differently. On my way to San Francisco my last job for Rio Tinto took me to the borax mine in the Mohave Desert to undertake a similar consultancy to the one at Rossing and Richards Bay Minerals.

Arriving in San Francisco around midnight, without a prepared sermon, I walked down at four in the morning to Fisherman's Wharf and suddenly the sermon and the future came to me clearly.

'Everything begins in the imagination,' wrote the poet William Blake. Albert Einstein said: 'Logic will get you from A to B; imagination will take you everywhere.'

The visit to the mine and working with the clergy at St Juan Capistrano had focused on the role of the imagination as a crucial agent for change: disrupting and destabilizing familiar and fixed ways of understanding. This disturbance provides an opportunity for seeing what could be.

My sermon put it like this:

The building of a New Europe is not just a matter for politicians and businessmen. Other voices need to be heard: poets and artists, theologians and philosophers, women, those who speak for the poor, and on behalf of the environment. These voices together with Christian, Muslim and Jewish communities articulate the soul of Europe.

The sermon concluded with a reminder that for ancient Israel the Bible tells stories of God who makes promises and keeps them, promises given in the most difficult and hopeless situations: of which the story of the elderly Abraham and Sarah where God says that barren Sarah will bear a child is the most striking. Sarah laughs; but Isaac and Jacob are born. St Paul's Letter to the Romans reflects on that same story: this God in whom Israel believes 'gives life to the dead and calls into existence the things that do not exist' (Romans 4, verse 17).

Our search for funds began with a stroke of good luck. Lord Plumb, then President of the European Parliament, knew St James's Piccadilly and wanted to encourage any initiatives which raised the profile of Europe in Britain, where most people resisted being part of the European Union. 'I am a European first,' he declared publicly, 'and British second.' He particularly appreciated the words from my sermon in San Francisco and offered to introduce me to the Duke of Westminster.

Unprepared for the meeting, arranged at short notice, and not having worked out a clear strategy, I expected nothing. All I could tell the Duke of Westminster was that the Soul of Europe intended to visit Serbia, then the pariah of Europe, shamed by its brutal part in the Bosnia War, and still in the grip of President Milošević and his cabal of extreme nationalists. Serbia had been bombed recently by NATO to force a rapid end to their ethnic cleansing of Muslims in Kosovo. We believed that the first duty of the Soul of Europe should be to visit the darkest place of our continent, meet people, listen, investigate, learn and see what we could do.

'What will be the outcome of your visit?' he asked.

'I have no idea,' I replied candidly.

After an embarrassing pause, sure I had blown it and wanting to make agreeable conversation, I told him: 'I used to be an officer cadet at Eaton Hall, during my National Service.' Eaton Hall was the Duke of Westminster's residence. I told him I used to play the organ for services in the chapel. The duke immediately showed interest. He said how much the chapel meant to him and his family.

He then brought the meeting to an end saying: 'I will match whatever you can manage to raise in four months.'

By 1st January 2000 we had eighty thousand pounds in the bank and the Soul of Europe embarked on its first project.

The visit to Serbia led to the Soul of Europe's first initiative, which culminated a year and a half later in September 2001: thirty leaders from Bosnia gathered at the International Centre for Reconciliation at Coventry Cathedral for a three-day consultation: 'Banja Luka – Beyond Conflict: Steps Towards Peace, Prosperity and Reconciliation'. The Soul of Europe funded, arranged and organized the event, hosted by Canon Andrew White, who has since become Vicar of Baghdad.

The successful outcome of this event put the Soul of Europe on the map.

An account of how Peter and I arrived at Banja Luka in Bosnia can be read in *A Tender Bridge*. Our journey took us first to Belgrade where we met Patriarch Pavle. I forgot to bring a gift and letter of commendation from the Archbishop of Canterbury. Flustered I also forgot the formal language required when meeting an Orthodox Patriarch. So I spoke simply and directly about the aims of the Soul of Europe. The old man smiled and we had two further meetings with him. He agreed to organize a public gathering of the religious leaders, Orthodox, Catholic, Jewish and Muslim, in the Patriarchate to show the world that despite the war which had torn the former country of Yugoslavia apart, the faith communities continued to build positive relationships. With the blessing of these leaders, whom we had also met separately, Patriarch Pavle sent us to Bosnia where they all agreed we could be most useful: helping the process of healing after the horrors of ethnic cleansing.

Our plan was to bring young people from all over Europe, of every faith and of none, to reconstruct an Orthodox church, a Catholic church and a mosque in Bosnia, where all three had been destroyed by war.

Meanwhile we visited France, Germany, Finland, Austria and Denmark looking for support and finding none. No one expressed any interest. The idea of reconstructing religious buildings had no resonance. We were also told to learn more about the political realities in Bosnia and come up with a more concrete proposal.

The reality of life in Bosnia on our subsequent visit did put the project on hold. There were more urgent matters that demanded immediate attention and action: the plight of refugees and returnees, displaced people, the collapse of the economy, corruption, the absence of justice, and the continued flourishing of those extreme nationalist movements which had so recently fought each other with shocking brutality. The Bosnia War might have been brought to an end on paper, with the Dayton Accord, but little had been solved and the war continued in people's heads.

This learning began to clarify the aims of the Soul of Europe. From being a means of establishing a Christian European network we moved towards projects and activities which focused on peace building.

More significantly, the Soul of Europe discovered that a major issue in Bosnia was the relationship between Europe and Islam, between East and West. The fault line ran through the Balkans, so this area became for the next eight years the centre of our activity. It was a striking coincidence that our first project culminated in the Consultation at Coventry in the same month, September 2001, when the terrorist attack on the World Trade Center alerted the whole world to this issue.

A Tender Bridge: Peace Building in the Balkans

Entering Northern Bosnia from Zagreb, the road narrows and crosses a plain towards Banja Luka. Peter described our first impression of Banja Luka in A *Tender Bridge* in June 2000.

We arrived at Banja Luka in the early evening, the hills rising behind the town, thickly forested, the scene reminding me of the lower foothills of the Alps in Austria. There is no sign of tourism and farms and small villages are scattered over the slopes. The sun set behind the western hills and the streets teemed with young people socializing in the cool of the evening.

Banja Luka is mostly a twentieth-century town with typically plain communist architecture, concrete tower blocks standing in rows against the wooded slopes. The wide, deep, cool River Vrbas flows through the town centre. A castle with a restaurant perches on a rock immediately above a bend in the river, providing a splendid view. In the Guide to Eastern Europe Banja Luka boasts the alarming qualification of being the least desirable place to visit in Easter Europe. For all its neglect and the terrible history of the last decade, including the destruction of all its mosques and the persecution of Muslims and Catholics, the evidence of this deliberate policy of obliteration has been comprehensively erased and the town gives an impression of peace and activity.[16]

Banja Luka is the administrative centre of the Republika Srpska, the Serb entity of Bosnia, roughly half of the country. The Republika Srpska was created by Radovan Karadžić in 1992 and ratified by NATO in the Dayton Accord. Muslims and Croats had constituted half of the Banja Luka population before the Bosnia War. Between 1992 and 1995 non-Serbs were systematically ethnically cleansed, harassed, humiliated, beaten and tortured, forced to flee and become refugees elsewhere in the world, or killed; their fate parallel to Jews in Germany during the Second World War. Elderly Muslims who could not flee were murdered in their homes; others hid in the woods and hills around the city to avoid being transported to the killing camps at Prijedor and Omarska. Six Catholic priests and nuns were murdered. Catholic churches were torched and all the mosques in the region razed to the ground and the rubble cleared to remove all traces of them. These included masterpieces of Ottoman architecture, the Ferhadija and Arnaudija Mosques in Banja Luka.

We arrived in Banja Luka unknown and uninvited. Then we returned again and again to invite people to the Coventry Consultation. We replaced our Serb interpreter and guide from Belgrade; he had offended the mufti of Banja Luka by telling him not to exaggerate Muslim suffering, and thereby almost capsized our project before it had started. We replaced him with Adnan Jabucar, a BBC trained journalist from Sarajevo, a Muslim who related well with

Serbs and Croats. His girlfriend was a Catholic and many of his best friends were Serbs. Adnan was pivotal to the project. His 'eyes' and 'ears' and contributions at meetings were essential. Peter, Adnan and I formed the small team which prepared the Coventry Consultation in September 2001. But we had the backing of the British Ambassadors in Sarajevo: first Graham Hand, then Ian Cliff and then Matthew Rycroft. Their advice helped us and we were also able to brief them.

We were also lucky to have the active support of Roy Wilson. He was head of the British Embassy office in Banja Luka. He went out of his way to help us, opening doors, arranging meetings with the president, prime minister and leading officials of the Republika Srpska, the Mayor of Banja Luka and his cabinet. Roy Wilson arranged for me to address the National Assembly, the parliament of the Republika Srpska, where for the first time since the war, nationalist politicians, instead of being harangued and criticized by international leaders, heard a foreigner invite them positively to improve the standing of their city by making reparations for war crimes and rebuilding the Ferhadija Mosque.

The reconstruction of the Ferhadija Mosque became a flagship project for the Soul of Europe. It was designed by Sinan, the great Ottoman architect. Together with the Mostar Bridge and the National Library in Sarajevo, the Ferhadija Mosque represented the best of Bosnia's cultural heritage. Mufti Čamdžić of Banja Luka in a long black coat and fez invited us into a small dilapidated building, the Islamic Centre, all that was left on the piece of waste ground where the Ferhadija Mosque had once stood. The mufti, looking like a rugged farmer used to working in the fields, listened to me talking about the Soul of Europe. He then told us about the ethnic cleansing of non-Serbs, the killing camps and the destruction of all the mosques in the Republika Srpska, including fifteen in Banja Luka. Without hesitation I promised the mufti that we would help him rebuild the Ferhadija Mosque. That momentous decision determined the course of the Soul of Europe. We intended the reconstruction of the mosque to be a means of bringing together all the faiths and so become a sign of reconciliation for Europe and beyond.

Over ten months we made eight visits. We got to know the Orthodox Bishop of Banja Luka, Bishop Jefrem. A supporter of Radovan Karadžić, he said that if the Bosnian Serb leader were ever caught and imprisoned he would be considered a martyr and saint. The Catholic Bishop of Banja Luka, Bishop Komarica, became a close friend. Together with Mufti Čamdžić and the two bishops we invited senior politicians, the mayor of Banja Luka, his cabinet, teachers and businesspeople to the Coventry Consultation.

Initially no one knew what to make of us. We did not arrive with a cheque book; we were not a proselytizing organization. We were not journalists. We were not academics researching on trauma in post-conflict situations. We were not working for the United Nations. We were not employed by the British government. We were not spies, although there was a rumour we worked for the CIA. We were always received politely. Once when I tried to rush discussion at a meeting in the mayor's office, the mayor of Banja Luka reprimanded me saying: 'hospitality first!'

We had to create sufficient trust so that all the people we invited would accept our invitation to Coventry. Everyone expressed interest, but only the Vice-President of the Republika Srpska formally accepted the invitation. We delivered the tickets personally two weeks before the Consultation. Roy Wilson fast-tracked the visas. We waited for the participants to arrive at Heathrow, almost deserted after 9/11 a week earlier. Was anyone going to come?

The Consultation could not have taken place nor had any success without the presence of Bishop Jefrem, the Orthodox Bishop of Banja Luka. He represented the majority in the city, and his authority went beyond that of politicians.

Though initially welcoming, in traditionally generous Bosnian style, the bishop was non-committal; even disinterested. 'I will need to pray about this,' he responded to my invitation to the Consultation. 'I already have,' I immediately told him, 'and you are coming.' At the next visit he dodged the invitation by saying he needed a formal written invitation from the Bishop of Coventry. We arranged this within three days. At the next visit he said: 'I am very busy, I cannot come.' At which point I knelt down in front of him and asked for his blessing. This took him by surprise. He could not refuse. After a moment's hesitation he solemnly gave me a blessing from the Orthodox liturgy. He then helped me to my feet and we could tell his attitude had softened. Without saying anything he implied a readiness to accept our invitation.

Back in England we began to receive messages from the bishop saying again that he could not come. I asked to meet the Bosnian Ambassador in London. Standing in his office I announced: 'In so far as you have no control over institutions in your country, I want to complain in the strongest possible terms about the behaviour of the Bishop of Banja Luka. Unless I hear from him within twenty-four hours I will inform the United Nations, the prime minister, Her Majesty the Queen, the World Council of Churches and the Patriarchate in Belgrade.'

I had played my last card. The next day I received a message from the Bosnian Embassy that the bishop would be coming to Coventry.

After my announcement to the ambassador there followed a flurry of calls to Banja Luka. The Vice-President of the Republika Srpska persuaded the bishop to change his mind – otherwise, he said, there would be 'an international incident'.

With the exception of two Muslim politicians, whom the National Assembly of Banja Luka prevented from coming, everyone we invited arrived. As soon as we saw the tall, lean bearded Bishop Jefrem in his black cassock at the arrivals entrance in Terminal 2, Heathrow, we knew that the Consultation was going to work.

Peter Ashby, Director of the 2 Way Trust, orchestrated the Consultation.[17] He rightly forced the pace, getting people to meet in pairs, then in smaller groups, with occasional plenary sessions. All of the issues facing Bosnia were raised. On two occasions Mufti Čamdžić and another mufti, Mufti Mahić from Bihać, whom we had specially invited so that Mufti Čamdžić would not be isolated in the mostly Serb Orthodox group, threatened to walk out.

At the end of the Consultation, relieved that we had reached the end without too much acrimony, I invited the participants, various VIPs from Bosnia, including the High Representative Wolfgang Petritsch, and the international press to give three cheers for the people of Bosnia. Hip Hip Hooray is not a Bosnian custom. They joined in uncertainly. We did it again and that was better!

The Prime Minister of the Republika Srpska, Mladen Ivanić, who came to the last day's session, echoed the thoughts of our own government as well as representatives of the international community in Bosnia, journalists and everyone who had watched our efforts with cynical scepticism. He had considered the Consultation to be a waste of time, but now had to admit: 'This was a big success.'

The Ferhadija Mosque still waits for reconstruction; but as I write, the foundations have been prepared, the stones cleaned and the government of the Republika Srpska, representing the same people who were responsible for its destruction, has made a substantial donation towards the cost.

All those who took part look back fondly to that time when at last they learned to speak with each other again. None more than Bishop Jefrem himself, who told us later that the Consultation had been one of the most important experiences of his life, as it was for me and for the Soul of Europe.

After Coventry the Soul of Europe intended to keep up the momentum to continue our work.

On our return to Banja Luka we invited the participants to meet again. They looked at us expectantly. We had invited them to see what practical steps they could take together and individually, to act on the resolutions agreed at the Consultation. Nothing had happened. They were expecting me to arrive with instructions. I had underestimated their fatalism, inertia and exhaustion. They were simply not able or ready to take initiatives.

Therefore we embarked on the task we began in Coventry, setting up informal conversations and meetings which we hoped would end in some sort of reconciliation, when, as the Catholic bishop told me: 'We will recognize we are neighbours.'

Funding for the Soul of Europe's work then became pressing.

The Foreign Office initially declined to make any funding available for Coventry, although Ambassador Graham Hand in Sarajevo gave a donation from his discretionary fund. But the World Islamic

Call Society, a Libyan organization, heard about our mission to improve relations between Islam and the West. Appreciating our support for the Islamic community in Bosnia they gave a substantial donation towards the costs of the Consultation. Without the help from Libya the Consultation would have had to be cancelled.

Then the British government's hospitality department sprang into action, not to pay for the Consultation itself but to provide stretch limos, dinner at the Connaught Hotel in London and a trip to Warwick Castle for Bosnian VIPs, politicians from both the Republika Srpska and the Muslim-Croat Federation, whom we had invited to attend the final day. I noted how the cost of that lavish hospitality could have kept our small organization going for a year.

However, when the Foreign Office witnessed our success they supported us willingly for one year, then, recognizing that our work was demanding more patience and time, less willingly for a further year.

We proposed establishing a Civic Forum in Banja Luka, based loosely on the model of the now defunct Scottish Civil Forum. The objective was to breathe life into a fledgling democracy: 'Real change happens when those who do not usually speak are heard by those who do not usually listen.' I hoped the forum would stir the people in Banja Luka out of their inertia and depression.

Once the forum had been established we submitted a bid for funding to the European Initiative for Democracy and Human Rights.

What followed is familiar to all those organizations who try to bring about change and come up against the bureaucracies of government and international institutions.

I delivered the sixty-page application to the European Commission in November 2002. Only in October 2003 did we learn that the bid, though marked at 85 per cent, had failed.

A particularly frustrating aspect of applying for funding from the European Commission forbids applicants personal contact with anyone connected with the bid. The Commission reasons that lack of personal contact prevents opportunity for bribery of officials. Queries can be submitted to an email address, but this contact vanished the moment the deadline passed. The Commission preserves distance between potential recipients and donors.

The way applications are framed and evaluated renders human contact and communication unnecessary.

The application reasonably demands a statement of aims, objectives and strategy. Then the demands intensify. Activities have to be described in detail. A three-year project requires a thorough analysis of activities from month to month; each activity has to relate to what precedes it and what follows. As the plan unfolds, so arrangements have to be put in place for internal and external continual assessment. Local partners have 'to provide value', and their 'performances' marked. Every activity had to relate to every other activity so that they could be brought together and placed in a logical framework. It was like doing a jigsaw puzzle. Any piece missing, the Commission warned me, and 'Your application will be binned.'

Such demands and information for projects like building bridges or a housing development are reasonable. But technical, financial grids for engaging in peace building and reconciliation do not fit.

Seven months after submitting the application, our friends in Banja Luka were waiting to know how the Civic Forum could proceed. Having heard nothing I called the European Commission. Friendly and polite officials passed me down the line, all scrupulously ignoring my questions. At the end of a fruitless three hours on the phone they put me through to a Spanish woman who screamed at me: 'I am not allowed to talk to you; I am not allowed to talk to anyone!'

On eventually hearing of the failure of our bid I managed to persuade the officials at the European Commission to meet me and explain why despite our high marking we had been rejected. An official showed me the report with the names of the evaluators blocked out. Most applications are marked at 40 per cent or 45 per cent, so 85 per cent would normally pass. The only reason they could give was the Soul of Europe's lack of experience in managing a large budget, to which I said: 'You only had to call the Bishop of London and he would have told you that St James's Piccadilly ran several successful business operations on a far larger budget.'

The Civic Forum foundered as a result of this decision. Ashamed about the delay and failure of the bid I met the partners in Banja Luka to pass on the bad news. They said: 'What do you expect? It's Europe.'

If I knew then what I know now, I would want to say to the UK government and the European Union:

Thank you for your encouragement. Now we must work together and with those who came to Coventry to see what we can do. We recognize this will take time, and there should be no pressure to come up with a programme. We shall first ask the questions: What changes happened at the Consultation or did not happen? What unexpected insights have we gained along the way that have nothing to do with our original proposal? Could we agree not to use words like impact, targets, log frames, delivery? Could we use plain English? We recognize that public money has to be accounted for in a transparent way. Could we therefore develop criteria for assessing the kind of work the Soul of Europe is doing (and countless others involved in peace building) which fit the processes that we use?

Following the Coventry Consultation and the setting up of the Banja Luka Civic Forum the Soul of Europe was asked to intervene in a situation which threatened to destabilize North Western Bosnia.

In 2005 a multinational mining company had acquired an iron ore mine in Omarska, near Prijedor, a town in the North of Bosnia two hours' drive from Zagreb in Croatia. This mine had been the site of a killing camp during the diligently planned programme of ethnic cleansing put into action at the beginning of the Bosnia War in 1992. All non-Serbs were removed from their jobs, forced to flee the country or imprisoned in killing camps. Serbs set up an alternative administration in the region. During the months May to August 1992 between three and four thousand people were murdered in the Prijedor region. In August 1992 Ed Vulliamy, the *Guardian* correspondent, discovered and reported the existence of the Omarska killing camp. In the Prijedor region not fewer than three thousand and not more than four thousand people were murdered. The exact numbers are not known. Some died at Omarska. Many more were tortured and raped and all kinds of atrocities inflicted.

The new mine owners began to receive demands from the survivors of the killing camp in the mine that a memorial be erected to those who died and suffered there. However, Serbs who now managed the mine insisted that despite all the evidence, no crimes had been committed there, and refused to permit a memorial. But the survivors persisted. More Muslims were returning to the region, and the weight of numbers and persistence of survivors' demands threatened the smooth operating of the mine.

So the new mine owners called us in to mediate between the various parties and reach an outcome which would satisfy the survivors, the Serb management, the predominantly Serb local authorities and the company headquarters in Rotterdam.

We had to consider carefully before accepting this invitation, knowing that the interests of the company and the mine management were limited to minimizing disruption of work and productivity, whereas our project had wider objectives. But the opportunity of continuing those aims we set out at the Coventry Consultation persuaded us to take the job on.

To ease the tension between the communities around the mine we brought Serbs and Bosnians together, beginning in groups of two, then four, and eventually up to sixty people were involved. A small but committed group of Serbs and Bosnians took over the project so that it continues beyond our remit. The process: discovering and encouraging allies, noting those who would have nothing to do with the project, dealing with an ambivalent international community, is described in *the white house: From Fear to a Handshake*, which Peter and I wrote subsequently.[18] (The white house is a shed on the edge of the mine complex where interrogation, atrocities and murder took place.)

The image that illustrates best the work of the Soul of Europe is of people facing each other round a circle, listening intently to each other's stories. This happened at Coventry, in the early days of the

Banja Luka Civic Forum and during the long process for establishing a memorial at Omarska.

Peace building is neither glamorous nor media-friendly. Our role is modest. Sometimes we are catalysts bringing people together to encourage their collaboration. Sometimes we are mediators directly bringing former enemies together, trying to interrupt the demonizing of each other. Sometimes we initiate projects, inviting key leaders in a region together as at Coventry, or encouraging the reconstruction of the Ferhadija Mosque, or setting up the Banja Luka Civic Forum.

Our role is modest, because we are guests of another country. Bosnia is not our land. Many of our friends respected our commitment: 'You guys are different; you keep on turning up,' they told us. The work we do whether in Bosnia or anywhere else has to be taken forward by the people themselves.

Progress is always slow, one step forward and several steps back. Governments are impatient; they dislike open-ended projects. They want projects 'done and dusted' with precise outcomes, delivered on time. Would that reconciliation were so straightforward.

When Patriarch Pavle sent the Soul of Europe to Bosnia we met all the religious leaders, the Catholic and Orthodox bishops, the Grand Mufti, Reis ul Ulema, of Bosnia and many muftis and imams. We have got to know some of them well and consider each our friend. But we would tell them from the start: 'We want to be useful to you, but that will not stop us being useful to others.'

Secular Europe underestimates the political and social significance of religion and religious leaders in the Balkans. In their person, by virtue of their office, they cradle the nationalistic mindset of their ethnic group. If nationalism is to be dismantled then that process has to start with the Orthodox bishops, the Catholic hierarchy and the Muslim imams. That is why it was essential to ensure Bishop Jefrem's presence at Coventry.

At the start of the Omarska project we accepted Bishop Jefrem's invitation to attend the consecration of the new Orthodox church in Omarska, a village adjacent to the mine. The entire village community of around four hundred people turned out along with many hundreds of Serbs from the surrounding region. The bishop arrived with a retinue of cantors, acolytes and priests carrying his vestments on coat hangers. On the chancel step sat three bells garlanded with flowers: the donors of the bells were presented to the bishop and the three-hour liturgy began. A chair had been provided for me. There were people considerably older than me standing so I stood. The bells were blessed and taken away to be hung in the belfry.

Following the liturgy we were invited to the banquet in a marquee next to the church. During the banquet the church bells peeled. Everyone stood in silence. The children playing outside stopped. The bells were a political statement. Under Muslim Ottoman rule over several centuries before the First World War the ringing of bells had been forbidden. Bishop Jefrem presided at the banquet. His presence proclaimed: 'This is now our land, our home, we are in charge.' A Serb told me: 'Take away our land and we are nothing.'

Our presence was appreciated by the management of the mine sitting at the top table with the bishop. Witnessing our readiness to listen and learn they began to trust us and agreed to take part in the memorial project.

The next day we attended the funeral of forty Muslims a few miles from Omarska whose bodies had been discovered in a mass grave along with four hundred other bodies still to be identified. During the dignified solemn ceremony at which the crowd of grief stricken mourners remained absolutely silent a mufti delivered a passionate sermon about the need for justice. Observing us in the crowd the muftis and imams, knowing about our work on the memorial project at the mine, were pleased we had made the effort to attend the ceremony.

During the war Bishop Jefrem was silent. Had he spoken up on behalf of non-Serbs his life would have been threatened.

The Mufti of Banja Luka died, it was said, from a broken heart after the destruction of the Ferhadija Mosque.

The Catholic Bishop Komarica stood up for victims from all three communities. This modest man of remarkable courage refused to leave Banja Luka when he could have fled to Croatia to sit out the war in Zagreb. While Serbs decimated his diocese he remained under house arrest for a year and converted the bishop's house into a clinic, open to all. He was fearless in the face of constant threats to his life. He told us: 'They would telephone me at three in the morning: we are coming to get you. They kidnapped and beat me many times. But I had to stay and speak up for the people.'

He took us to Presnace, a village close to Banja Luka. On 12th May 1995 Serb militia destroyed the church. They forced their way into the priest's house and ordered the parish priest Father Philip Lukenda to rape a nun, Sister Cecilia Grgic, who worked in the parish. He of course refused and both were shot and the bodies burned. Sister Cecilia had been at her convent in Zagreb the day before and the Sisters had begged her not to return to Presnace. But she insisted. 'I have to be with my people,' she said.

Today the room in the priest's house where they were murdered is a shrine to the memory of Father Philip and Sister Cecilia. The floor is still stained with their blood. This is a sacred site, a place of silence, grace and healing. The church has been rebuilt by the whole local community, including Orthodox Serbs and Muslims, as a sign of reconciliation hardly known in Bosnia let alone the rest of Europe.

Bosnia has a thousand-year history of conflict between the Catholic and Orthodox Churches, more intense than between Christianity and Islam. During the Second World War, Catholic Croats, fascist allies of the Nazis, committed atrocities against Orthodox Serbs. The Pope, then John Paul II, had visited Croatia and Sarajevo; we agreed with Bishop Komarica that if the Pope came to Banja Luka his visit could begin to heal deep wounds. I went to Rome and spoke with the Papal Secretary who arranges the Pope's journeys. 'There are witnesses to the faith in North West Bosnia,' I told him. 'Six priests and one nun have been murdered and many tortured and raped. I know the Holy Father has been to Sarajevo; now he must come to Banja Luka.' The Secretary said: 'The Catholic Church there is lucky to have good friends like you who care for it.' I responded forcefully: 'It is not up to me to do this. The Catholic Church has to take responsibility. The people there need to know they have not been abandoned.'

Some months later when I returned to Banja Luka, Bishop Komarica greeted us warmly as always and said laughing: 'You must have said something in the Vatican. The Pope has changed his mind. He is coming.'

At the Papal Mass held in a field outside Banja Luka, where once Catholics had murdered Orthodox Serbs, the Pope asked for forgiveness for crimes committed in the name of his Church. Bishop Komarica called me up to the platform afterwards, along with Mufti Čamdžić, to receive a blessing from the now ailing pontiff. His illness made it difficult for him to move but he held my hand tightly and stared searchingly into my eyes.

We tried and sometimes succeeded in bringing the religious groups together with their leaders. We drafted a statement together with Bishop Jefrem, Bishop Komarica and Mufti Čamdžić expressing opposition to the Iraq War. This was widely publicized. But mutual suspicion persists. Orthodox Serbs remember the massacre of Serbs in the Second World War; Catholics remember Orthodox religious leaders colluding in the persecution and killing during the Bosnia War; Muslims trust neither and are trusted by neither Orthodox nor Catholics. But I am invited to speak at Friday Prayers in mosques and to preach at the Catholic Mass and at the Orthodox Liturgy.

Nationalism will not be dismantled until the truth of what happened during the Bosnia War is established and that truth has to recognize the part played by religion.

Small Is Beautiful: Working in the Church of England

Once I was invited by the Cambridge Business School to give an after-dinner talk to a group of top executives from Shell BP. 'Twenty minutes max,' I was told. 'Keep it light.' I spoke for forty minutes about the Soul of Europe's work with our small team of five in Bosnia.

Subsequently half a dozen people asked to have a private conversation. They said the same thing: 'I am well paid, good pension and benefits. But I am trapped, powerless. I would really like to quit.'

These conversations and many like them when I was a consultant at Rio Tito point one way: 'We do not like working in large organizations.'

I had been a parish priest for thirty years. I appreciated working in a small organization, although in Piccadilly our organization was problematic. Eventually up to a dozen people were employed full time. Then there were paid part timers, voluntary part timers, students on placement, full-time volunteers and from time to time invited visitations by paid consultants. Sometimes, talking about St James's Piccadilly, I made a point of saying what a large staff there was. I do not think anyone was impressed.

The parish is the key unit in the Church of England. In theory the diocese and the organization of the national Church exist to serve the parishes. In practice this does not happen.

In 1989 five vicars of five parishes in Central London met to see how we could secure the cooperation of the Diocese of London. We were Christopher Hamel Cooke of Marylebone Parish Church, Geoffrey Brown at St Martin-in-the-Fields, Victor Stock of St Mary le Bow, Malcolm Johnson of St Botolph's Aldgate and myself. We were impatient at the lack of response from the bishop to significant activities in our parishes, some involving considerable sums of money for development, applications for faculties with threats of litigation and consistory courts. Trust between the bishop and the diocese had broken down. We were angry. Collectively we felt we were regarded as a nuisance. We even considered strike action. Eventually the bishop agreed to a meeting and some progress was made.

The problems were not just a matter of personalities. It was the lack of any intermediary organization between the diocese and the parishes.

Our problem in Central London in the late 1980s is a sign of the top heavy organization of the Church of England.

In 1900 there were fifty-seven bishops (thirty-one diocesan and twenty-six suffragan) and twenty-four thousand clergy. In 2008 there are one hundred and thirteen bishops (forty-four diocesan and sixty-nine suffragan) and nine thousand full-time licensed clergy (although there are unpaid and retired priests, but the full-time number is the key figure).

The Archbishop's Council was established to 'provide a focus for leadership and executive responsibility and a forum for strategic thinking and planning. Within an overall vision of the Church set by the House of Bishops, the Council will propose an ordering of priorities in consultation with the House of Bishops and the General Synod and to be an overview of the Church's financial needs and resources.'

As I write, a review is being undertaken to see if the Council is 'delivering what stakeholders wanted, high quality, cost effective work for the mission of the Church of England'.

Renewal for the Church will not emerge from mission statements of 'visions' from the hierarchy. In the nineteenth century the renewal of Anglicanism came from the Evangelical Revival and the Oxford Movement. Today renewal is emerging from a variety of evangelical groups and in networks like Affirming Catholicism, the Modern Churchperson's Union, the Inclusive Churches Network, Progressive Christianity and Fresh Expressions, which are 'forms of church for our changing culture, established for those who are not members of any church'.

If history is any guide, the transformation of the Church of England will begin at the grass roots. Church goers are already pressed to give more time and money. They do not respond enthusiastically to the business-speak of the Archbishop's Council.

To support the parishes, power, resources and authority need to be taken by local churches, through the deanery, to manage their own affairs.

Bureaucracy needs to be trimmed. The number of bishops should be reduced. The Archbishop's Council should be dismantled. Local resources need to be carefully guarded. The sale of rectories and vicarages should be stopped. With a little ingenuity these properties can be useful for local churches and local communities. Thus the organization of the Church of England needs to be reversed: lean at the top and filled out locally. In some parts of Britain there is a demand for hospitals and schools to be locally controlled. Why cannot the Church of England locally control its own affairs?

Many clergy of my generation look with dismay, not just at a top heavy church but with its changing character.

Historically Anglican churches have been and still are what the writer Simon Jenkins has called the nation's most visible public institutions and so are the natural centres for social action. He writes:

With the dismantling of local political responsibility by the Thatcher and Blair regimes, churches have stood increasingly alone in poor communities. Priests are often the only professionals still resident in inner city estates. They are informal mayors, social workers, marriage counsellors, police and conciliators.[19]

These are just the sort of priests for which the Urban Ministry Project existed.

Now there is much at stake for the Church of England which has long been a significant part of British history and culture.

Conservative evangelicals have a different agenda. Their priority is church planting and building up committed congregations. St Peter's Morden, for example, which had traditionally been a central part of the social life of the St Helier Estate, now has a mission statement: 'Making Jesus the heart of our community'.

There is a danger that our inheritance is being lost or betrayed. One of the success stories of the Church of England is the work of the Church Urban Fund, arising directly from the Faith in the City Report of 1985. Eighteen million pounds was raised 'to serve the poorest in society' in three years from 1988 to 1991. And in twenty years sixty million pounds have funded five thousand local projects in the poorest urban areas in England. What could happen if the Church Urban Fund was to be infiltrated and taken over? If this is not to sound like scaremongering then evangelical bishops should state unequivocally their solidarity with this inheritance as bishops in the Church of England and to see their actions match their words.

What the Church of England will look like in fifty years I cannot tell. One thing is certain: I will not be here to witness its dying or its rebirth.

PART THREE

Work in Progress

'When are you going to slow down?' asked my cousin Susan as I was approaching my seventy-fourth birthday.

I said I already have. I am not as agile as I was when I was thirty but going to the gym three times a week has made me more mobile than when I was sixty.

At seventy-plus I am aware that sooner or later I will die. Nothing, not even working out at the gym, can contradict that fact.

The universe is indifferent to our well-being; it is disinterested. For a long time I did not exist. I was not. Then for less than a flicker of an eyelid I am. Then I will be no more. Death is waiting as the Psalmist says: 'The days of our age are threescore years and ten; and though men be so strong that they come to fourscore years yet it is their strength then but labour and sorrow, so soon passeth it away, and we are gone.' (Psalm 90, verse 10)

Some will miss me. Like all partings, having to leave without any possibility of return is painful. At airports and railway stations I have wished the parting would happen quickly, but at the same time holding on for a moment, perhaps there is something more to say. For those who remain, parting is even more painful: memories are everywhere.

How well we die depends on how we live, barring the tragedy of accident or natural disaster, and if body and mind have not disintegrated too much.

Bessie Glover died well. She used to assist the housekeeper at

Bishop's House when Mervyn Stockwood entertained guests. Calm and efficient, she had been a cook and housekeeper all her life, helped prepare receptions at Edwardian house parties, and in her neat handwriting wrote down favourite recipes in exercise books, some of which she left me. After the meal I went to the kitchen at Bishop's House to take her home and would find her sitting there in hat and coat waiting. If I needed help entertaining at St Peter's, Bessie would come and take over the kitchen, making pies, preparing salads and whipping up orange mousses, the place a flurry of dishes and activity; then everything was tidied away as though she had never been there.

One day she arrived unannounced. She seemed nervous. 'I have just come to say thank you,' she said, and left. Two days later she died in her bed, falling asleep for the last time. The house was spotless and the fridge cleared. She had come to say good bye. She died naturally. She died as she had lived.

There is some comfort in recognizing that I am just one minute particle, one of at least sixty billion people who have passed before me. The indifferent universe will continue. I find comfort in the thought of my body being returned to the earth: 'Earth to earth, ashes to ashes, dust to dust' as the Order for the Burial of the Dead in the Book of Common Prayer puts it, and even more explicitly in the liturgy for Ash Wednesday: 'Dust thou art, and unto dust thou shalt return.'

But there is more to say. Richard Holloway, in *Looking in the Distance: The Human Search for Meaning*, describes the deep emptiness of an indifferent universe. Then he writes: 'as well as moments of deep emptiness, the mystery of Being affords fleeting moments of encounter with what feels like a kind of presence'. He continues:

'the moments are confronted by a certain gracious latency in creation, a sense of something not yet disclosed'.[1]

Those 'moments of encounter . . . confronted by a certain gracious latency in creation' disclose the source of the imagination. The imagination has been a recurring theme of this book and my life. The imagination is the source of creativity, of art and of religion. Above all the imagination is a gift. I would say a divine gift. It is not something invented; it is given. imagination is an act of grace; and it is as valid a way of knowing as the way of reason.

This gift evokes praise, gratitude, hope and love. Where it is bestowed, the air is 'thin' as at Presnace; heaven is close to the earth there.

There are those who live out of the imagination; they live 'as if' we are free, 'as if' justice can be done, 'as if' forgiveness is possible. The imagination rejects as false what has long been accepted and is beyond all criticism. A long-established 'as if' can keep people in their places until a counter 'as if' emerges, imagined and given a voice.

I willingly carry the bags for those who live 'as if' another world is waiting.

Here are two stories from Bosnia.

The ethnic cleansing of all non-Serbs in the northern regions of Bosnia included the attempt to remove all trace of the Catholic diocese of Banja Luka: priests, monks, nuns, people and churches. Convents became a particular target. In June 1992, after six months of harassment, Serb militia destroyed the parish house of Nova Topola, a small town to the north of Banja Luka, and took the priest, Father Ratko Grgic away. The priest was never seen again, presumed murdered along with five other Catholic priests. Then the nuns, mostly elderly, were physically and some sexually assaulted.

They were thrown on a lorry and driven to the border with Croatia and told to cross the bridge over the River Sava. 'You will never get there,' the Serbs told them, 'the bridge has been mined.' The nuns walked across the bridge, singing the Magnificat, and to the amazement of the militia, arrived unharmed on the other side.

After the war the nuns returned to their convent, to start repairing the severely damaged church and buildings. When I asked them why they had returned they told me: 'This is our home.' The Order of the Adorers of the Blood of Christ had been founded in 1834 as 'a reconciling presence for the poor in our midst'. In Nova Topola this meant running a small farm, teaching music, organizing sewing classes, providing health care and producing home grown herbal medicines for the local Serb population.

Serbs once again come to the now restored convent for advice and medicine. The Reverend Mother told me: 'They hold out their hands but do not look at us, bowing their heads in shame. We help them as much as we can. We just do our work. One day we may talk with them about what happened here.'

A United Nations peacekeeper, who supports the Soul of Europe's work, told me: 'I don't do nuns, Donald. Why do you support the losers?' I support them because they are an inspiration. I respect their hope and above everything their courage.

About thirty miles from the convent lives Mirsad Duratović, a Muslim survivor of the Omarska killing camp. Serb militia took the seventeen-year-old boy as a human shield to the camp along with his father and younger brother; he was compelled to watch them being murdered. After days of interrogation and torture he only avoided being shot because one of the Serbs took pity and hid him. After international outcry as a result of the journalist Ed Vulliamy's reports, the camp closed down and Mirsad was bussed to Croatia and from there made his way to Germany as a refugee. He worked as a labourer, and happened to meet another Bosnian refugee, a girl from his home village. They married and returned home as soon as they could after the end of the war. Mirsad is the only male survivor of his family; father, uncles, brother, cousins were all murdered. Now in his early thirties he rebuilds his life and home with wife, sister, mother and two sons.

Mirsad lives 'as if'. Talking about the people who tried to kill him, meeting and recognizing them every day on the street, the Serbs who murdered his uncles, he says: 'Sometimes I don't know if I can control myself. How long can we live with unpunished crimes?' But he discourages his sons from playing with toy guns: 'War is not the answer.' He also looks after the shattered community of Muslim returnees trying to rebuild homes and villages in this traumatized region of Bosnia. They appointed him community leader, to negotiate with the Serb-run local councils for water and electricity supplies which were still being denied ten years after the war ended. Recently he told me about the continuing antagonism between neighbouring communities. Serbs in the next village had blown up a bridge to prevent Muslims from reaching their fields at harvest. The Muslims wanted to retaliate by blowing up a Serb bridge. Mirsad calmed them. 'That is not the way. We have to live together.' His wisdom, dignity and humanity are an inspiration. Now he has been appointed chairman of the committee for the memorial at Omarska, and is a respected politician in the region's Serb administration.

Mirsad, the nuns of Nova Topola and countless others in Bosnia and elsewhere in the world live 'as if'; they are my teachers.

It is a mystery in the universe which is indifferent to our well-being that there are those who bother about their neighbour. Goodness is puzzling.

There is a vast inexhaustible reservoir to draw on which feeds the spirit: the Bible as I have come to appreciate it; above all the potent, extravagant, cosmic symbol, statement and fact of the Crucifixion and Resurrection: new life emerging, bursting forth.

There are echoes of these mysteries all around. Cormac McCarthy's *The Road* tells of a father and son walking alone through post-apocalypse USA. In this godforsaken landscape inhabited by men and women reduced to cannibalism, the father's love for his son shines: 'All things of grace and beauty such that one holds them to one's heart have a common provenance in pain. Their birth in grief and ashes. So, he whispered to the sleeping boy: I have you.'[2]

The reservoir holds memories of the Church's long history. Some of that history is a tale of oppression and collusion with evil in the name of God, but also memories of Exodus, Resurrection and possibilities of liberation. The reservoir holds a place of honour for those passionate men and women of all faiths and none, where the fire burns brightly; many of whom I know about, a few whom I have met and who are all my teachers.

The reservoir is filled with music, especially the music of Bach, and particularly what he wrote for the organ. I have played the organ intermittently for sixty years. After leaving Piccadilly I promised myself to learn all that Bach composed for the organ.

To be a musician demands time and determination, for an organist not least in finding an instrument to play. Churches do not always welcome organists, and create enough obstacles to discourage those with insufficient resolve. Once the almost impossible per-mission has been granted there are keys to find for opening doors, light switches to discover, coping with bone chilling unheated lofts in winter, choosing times when the church is not being used for services and choir practice, bell ringing . . .

But the hassle is worth it. The great cellist Pablo Casals described Bach as 'a volcano'. He was referring to the emotional content of Bach's music. Beyond the familiar *Toccata and Fugue in D minor* is a mighty range of organ compositions ranging from the majestic to the lyrical, from joy to despair, from suffering to rapture and seren-ity. Bach's music is brooding, exultant, defiant and soothing. Per-forming Bach as opposed to listening to him is like a home-coming for me. His compositions move through the knottiest complexities that reflect the vicissitudes of life and his music ends in a peace and harmony hard won, but as inevitable as the faith and hope which inspired and motivated him throughout his life.

The particular pleasure of learning to play Bach lies in the chal-lenge. Formidable technical difficulties seem to set the music beyond the player; then gradually as the fingers and feet come together and the problems are resolved the music begins to play itself . . . the music flies.

To return to my cousin's question 'When are you going to slow down?' the answer is: 'Not until I am physically incapable.' With such a reservoir to feed and nourish the imagination it would be inconceivable to stop. New work, new projects, new opportuni-ties present themselves continually, and big projects remain forever beyond completion, like the Promised Land out of Moses' reach.

It is unlikely I will see the result of much of the work I am doing, unfinished as it is. The theologian Reinhold Niebuhr wrote:

Nothing that is worth doing can be achieved in our lifetime; therefore, we must be saved by hope. Nothing which is true, or beautiful, or good, makes complete sense in any immediate context of history; therefore, we must be saved by faith. Nothing we do, however virtuous, could be accomplished alone; therefore, we must be saved by love.

Whether anything I have done makes a difference and contributes to the sum of wisdom I cannot tell. The point is to follow where the imagination beckons.

A rider passed a sparrow lying on its back with its feet in the air.

'What are you doing?' asked the rider.

'I've heard the sky is falling down today,' said the sparrow.

'Well,' said the rider, 'you are not going to make much difference.'

Said the sparrow: 'One does what one can.'

Appendix

FOR DONALD REEVES
Poem composed by Kathleen Raine for Donald's leaving St James's, Piccadilly

Dear Donald, casting our minds back, memories
And imagination, truest of records,
We bring, each of us, what we have at heart
Here and now together at St James's.

The last time comes, never as expected
Bringing full circle to completion the beginning:
You stood, raising in your hand the staff of office
And broke it in the name of William Blake,
Poet of this church, and of all London's sons and daughters.

With marks of weakness, marks of woe, he found us,
But you have taught us that in love there are no disbelievers,
Sceptic, drop-outs, cold perfectionists, our ordinary faces
Made beautiful and dear to one another
By unjudgmental love received and given.

I remember the day when we read in relay
The complete poems of Blake, remember
Concerts, poetry-reading, Tarkovsky who filmed the sacred
     vision,
Michael Horovitz blowing the ram's horn of Judah,
The High Commissioner of India planting in Blake's honour
The mulberry tree beside the Wren Café.

MEMOIRS OF A VERY DANGEROUS MAN

Here Trevor Huddleston found sanctuary
In his great battle for the soul of Africa,
Peter Pelz painted in triptych the transfiguration
Of our shabby world into the New Jerusalem,
Remember the Hare Krishna people serving curry and cups
    of tea,
The Findhorn people dancing.

And always, day and night, there would be someone
To listen to London's lost despairing night-wanderers
Bringing their hopelessness hoping for hope.
Here the hopeless from the winter cold found shelter.

Between Piccadilly and Jermyn Street
St James's has been our Ark, riding the flood of our
    times and places
And now as end and beginning meet full circle
All within that mandala is for ever, is Now, is timeless.
And what you have given us, Donald, is ours, and
    London's, always.

Kathleen Raine

Notes

PART ONE

1 AB GOURLAY. *A History of Sherborne School* (Warren 1951) page 179.

2 PETER LEWIS. 'Mummies, Matrons and the Maids: Feminine Presence and Absence in Male Institutions 1934–1963'. This essay appeared in *Manful Assertions: Masculinities in Britain Since 1800* (Routledge). Peter was a contemporary at Sherborne. I have drawn heavily from this essay for this section on my schooldays.

3 PETER DICKINSON. Composer, writer and pianist. Peter is Emeritus Professor at Keele University. He set up the Department and Centre for American Music in 1974. Among his CDs are his complete organ works, to be released on Naxos in 2009.

4 PAUL TILLICH. *The Shaking of the Foundations* (Penguin 1962)

5 FR LEAVIS. *The Common Pursuit* (Peregrine Books 1962)

6 TREVOR BEESON. *Round the Church in 50 Years* (SCM 2007) page 97.

7 TREVOR BEESON. *Round the Church in 50 Years* (SCM 2007). I want to acknowledge Trevor Beeson's help in this section. He conveys the flavour of the Church of England in the 1950s and early 1960s exactly as I recall it. There is a sympathetic vignette of St James's Piccadilly (p. 222) entitled: 'Openness, Struggle, Laughter and Prayer on Piccadilly' page 78.

8 MICHAEL DE LA NOY. *Mervyn Stockwood: A Lonely Life* (Mowbray 1996) page 49.

9 SEAN O'HAGAN. *Everyone to the Barricades* (*Observer*, 20th January 2008). I have quoted extensively from this *Observer* article: a succinct description of the year 1968.

10 RICHARD LUECKE. *Perchings* (Fortress Press 1972) page 8.

11 ALAN BENNETT. My notebook includes these words from Alan Bennett, but I cannot now find the source.

12 JULIA USHER. A versatile composer influenced by words and visual imagery, she has a particular interest in chamber music and writing for solo instruments. Julia works as a music therapist.

13 DAVID SCOTT. Rector of St Laurence with St Swithun's Winchester.

14 UMP. The Urban Ministry Project ended in 1984, with two courses for senior church leaders in collaboration with the William Temple Foundation.

PART TWO

1 HUGO YOUNG. *One of Us* (Macmillan 1989) page 380.

2 TREVOR BEESON. *Round the Church in 50 Years* (SCM 2007)

3 IVOR BOLTON. The two most prominent directors of music at St James's Piccadilly were Leopold Stokowski and Ivor Bolton. Ivor is the chief conductor of the Mozarteum Orchestra in Salzburg and a guest conductor at all the main world opera houses. In an interview in *Time Out* in May 2006 he said: 'I've a soft spot for St James's but I don't miss the eternal chaos of the organization.'

4 HENRI NOUWEN. *The Road to Daybreak* (Image 1990)

5 GILLIAN WEIR. Website: www.gillianweir.com

6 EF SCHUMACHER. *Small Is Beautiful* (Vintage 1993)

7 WALTER BRUEGGEMANN. *The Prophetic Imagination* (Augsburg Fortress 2nd Edition 2001). Walter Brueggemann's scholarship and insights into contemporary culture have been and continue to be energizing and inspirational.

8 WALTER BRUEGGEMANN. *Mandate to Difference* (Westminster Press 2007) page 192.

9 NANCY C LEE. *The Singers of Lamentations* (Brill 2002) By kind permission.

10 EDWIN MUIR. *Collected Poems* (Faber 1984)

11 ZAMANI SOWETO SISTERS COUNCIL. The Council established an umbrella organization of Soweto women's self-help groups.

12 MATTHEW FOX. *Original Blessings* (Tarcher/Putnam Edition 2000)

13 THEODORE ROSZAK. *The Making of a Counter Culture* (Faber 2000)

14 IAN McEWAN. *On Chesil Beach* (Vintage Books 2008) page 21.

15 WALTER BRUEGGEMANN. He has written extensively about

'land'. Some of this paragraph was inspired by *Interpretation and Obedience* (Augsburg Fortress 1991) page 235.

16 PETER PELZ. *A Tender Bridge: A Journey to Another Europe* (Cairns 2001) page 197.

17 PETER ASHBY – founder and director of the 2 Way Trust, whose aim is to support organizations in improving their business performance through leadership teams dealing with unhelpful behaviour. www.2waytrust.com

18 PETER PELZ. *The white house: From Fear to a Handshake* (O books 2008)

19 'Let a church so fond of division test its worth in the market place of belief.' (Simon Jenkins, *Guardian*, 4th July 2008)

PART THREE

1 RICHARD HOLLOWAY. *Looking in the Distance* (Cannongate Books 2004) page 54.

2 CORMAC McCARTHY. *The Road* (Picador 2006) page 56.

PHOTOGRAPH

'My father's garage bombed by the Germans – February 10th 1943.' Reproduced with permission from Bernard Price, Chichester. 'The Valiant Years', published by Phillimore & Co Ltd.

Index